How to Design Logos on your Computer

For Macintosh & PC Users

David E. Carter

©Copyright, 1993, Art Direction Book Co.

ISBN: 0-88108-117-5
LCCN: 93-071361

Art Direction Book Co.
10 E. 39th Street
New York, NY 10016
(212) 889-6500

This publication is designed to provide accurate and authoritative information in regard to the subject matter covered. It is sold with the understanding that the copyright holder is not engaged in rendering legal,or other professional service. If legal advice or other expert assistance is required, the services of a competent professional person should be sought.

Except where noted, the logos shown herein were created for the express purpose of showing examples of design possible by using a computer. In many cases, fictitious names of firms are used. No use of a design or name is intended to refer to an existing firm, nor is any endorsement or connection to such a real firm intended.

Any names of hardware or software products are the trademarks of their respective owners. No endorsement is implied.

How to Design Logos on Your Computer

Part 1: Fundamentals..........4

1. You can design great logos!..........5
2. Hardware and Software..........7
3. Before you start the design..........13
4. Setting design parameters..........23
5. Good logos and bad logos..........25
6. Selling and presenting your work..........33
7. Logo design: computer style..........38
8. Using type effectively..........47
9. Using Lines, Shapes & Color..........51
10. Designing a Stationery System..........57
11. Corporate ID Programs..........67
12. Legal aspects of logo design..........79

Part 2: Logo Examples..........81

13. Using the Computer tools to create logos..........83
14. Some logo design formats..........111

Part 3: Software You'll Want..........191

Add-Depth..........192
Adobe Dimensions..........194
Adobe Multiple Master Fonts..........196
Altsys Fontographer..........200
Bitstream Makeup..........202
Effects Specialist..........204
FontMonger..........206
Font Studio..........208
Letra Studio..........210
MenuFonts..........212
StrataType 3d..........214
The TypeBook..........216

TypeStyler..........218
Treacyfaces Typeface Collection..........220
Logo SuperPower..........222

Part 4: Sample Logo Design Project...........227

15. The Pinnacle Corporation Identity Program.....228

Chapter 1
You can design great logos!

Even if you're a novice, with little or no art skills, you can design logos like those shown here. Honest.

This book will tell you how to do it. With the right software, you'll be able to produce logos like these in a matter of minutes.

More great logos.

Here are some more outstanding logos which were created on a computer; they were also done in less than 4 minutes each.

Now that we have your attention with all the nice logos, we need to get technical for a chapter or two and talk about the tools you'll need to do great logos on your computer.

Chapter 2
Hardware & Software

We'll get back to the logo creation process in a few minutes. But for now, we have to give you some basic information about the hardware and software you'll need. (A lot of this is very basic stuff, so if you already have a computer with a PostScript® printer, skip to the "Software" section on the next page.)

Computer

For the novice, there are two basic types of computers: Apple **Macintosh** and IBM **PC** compatible. Each type computer has different operating systems, and generally speaking, Macintosh programs will not run on a PC, and vice versa.*

Printer

Until recently, you needed a PostScript® printer to print *type* with acceptable quality. A printer without PostScript would produce jagged edges on type. However, the introduction of TrueType fonts has changed all that. With TrueType, the jagged edges are eliminated. If you intend to produce camera-ready output from your printer, it's best to go with a higher resolution printer, such as 1,000 or 1,200 dots per inch (dpi). The graphics below show the difference between a 1,000 dpi printer and the 300 dpi models. I highly recommend LaserMaster's 1,000 dpi models.

Output on a 300 dpi printer   Output on a 1,000 dpi printer

•Actually, there is a program for the Macintosh that effectively allows a Mac to run PC programs. However, this is an expensive program, and many popular applications are available in both PC and Macintosh platforms.

Software

In order to create logos on your computer, you'll need to have a "drawing" program. The top-ranked programs for each platform are shown below.

Basic Drawing Programs

Macintosh	PC
•Aldus FreeHand •Adobe Illustrator •Canvas •Corel Draw	•Corel Draw •Micrografx Designer •Arts & Letters Editor •Adobe Illustrator •Aldus FreeHand •Artline

You'll notice that FreeHand, Illustrator and Corel Draw appear on both lists. A little background: When the Macintosh was introduced in the mid-1980s, it was designed with graphic applications in mind. Adobe Illustrator was the first "drawing" program for the Mac. It was followed shortly afterwards by Aldus FreeHand. Not long afterwards, Corel Draw was introduced for the PC. For several years, Illustrator and FreeHand dominated the Mac drawing market, while Corel Draw virtually owned the PC field.

With the massive growth of the computer field, though, Aldus FreeHand and Adobe Illustrator introduced PC versions, and in early 1993, Corel Draw introduced a Mac version.

Each of the programs listed above has its share of "evangelists" who swear by it. And all of them have many features in common with all the other drawing programs.

Drawing Program Design Features

(If you already have one of these programs, this section will only bore you. Skip ahead to the next chapter. You'll be one step closer to designing great logos.)

Virtually all of the programs listed on the previous page let you perform some specialized design functions. The "toolbox" lets you create "base object" shapes such as squares, rectangles, circles, ovals, round corner squares, etc., in just a second or two.

"Base Objects" created from the toolbox of a drawing program.

All of the drawing programs also let you create type, which may be integrated with any of the graphics crated on the screen.

9

The drawing programs will also let you change graphic (and type) shapes in ways such as stretching, condensing, rotating, skewing, copy and repeat, and blending.

Stretched
Stretched

Stretching

Condensed
Condensed

Condensing

Rotating

Skewing

Copy and Repeat

Blending

The drawing programs mentioned in this chapter can do all these things -- and many more. These are just a few of the techniques you'll be using as you create logos.

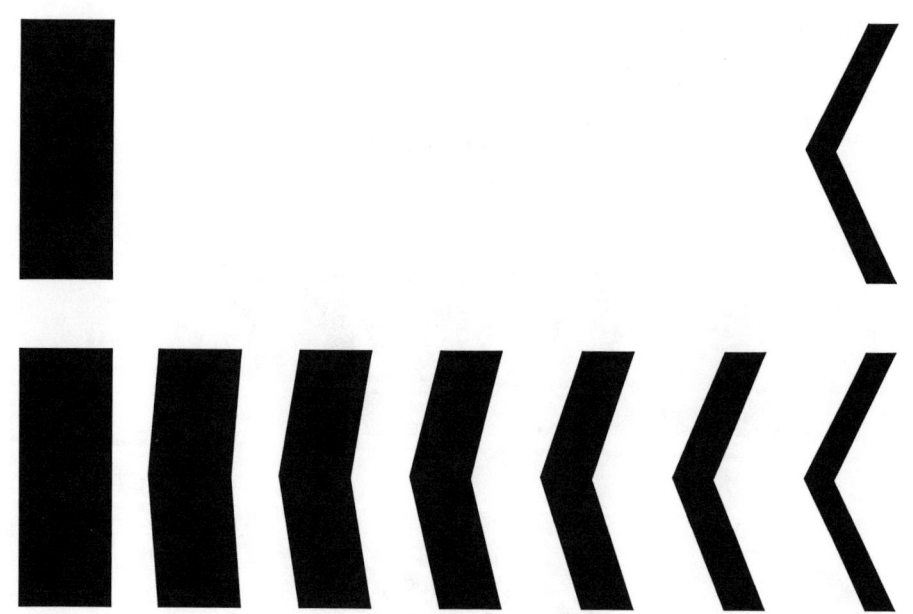

Blending Shapes

Type on a Curved Path

Chapter 3
Before you start the design...

When you begin a logo design project, your first instinct is to switch on the computer, fire up your favorite drawing program and put some graphics on the screen. That's not the way to do it.

Why? A logo is perhaps the most important part of any company's marketing program. If the logo is good, it's going to be used for a long time — maybe 20 years or more. It's going to be on virtually everything which displays the company's name: from stationery to vehicles to packaging to signage. The logo that you design is going to represent the client company as people see it thousands of times a day. The logo design must be a well-planned corporate visual statement, even for a small company. No, make that *especially* for a small company.

As a beginning logo designer, your target market is going to be small businesses. The typical small company doesn't have an excess amount of money to begin with. (Under-capitalization is cited as a major reason for small business failures.) The owner(s) are probably working more hours than they ever imagined. They have more responsibility than they really want. Their immediate and long-term futures depend upon the success of the business.

The typical small business doesn't have a big ad budget. ("We'll get our sales up," the owners say, "then we can spend some *big* money on advertising.") So how does anyone know about their company? From sales letters, the company's sign, its brochure (dropped off by a salesman) and ads. So, here are the primary corporate identity vehicles of most companies:

1. Letterhead, envelope and business card.
2. Sign
3. Brochure
4. Small space advertising

What do these items have in common? All of them include the company logo.

And most people who do see these items do not have any *personal* contact with the company. So, the logo is the one common element that is going to create a first impression with most of the company's prospects.

Take a look at the two logos below.

Which one looks like it's a successful company? The answer should be obvious. (If you aren't sure which logo is better, maybe you should see if your bookseller will give you a refund. You can say "I've hardly used it" and mean it.)

People don't want to do business with an unsuccessful company. (The only exception is at "going out of business sales" where they might pick up some bargains for a few bucks.) It's a fact of business life that in order to be successful, you have to *look* successful. The logo designer can play an important part in that success. You have a lot of responsibility in your hands. If your client runs a small ad that is a total failure, he simply doesn't run it again, and the damage is minimal. If you create a logo that doesn't portray the company properly, that wrong impression will persist in the minds of people for a long time — for as long as the logo is in use.

Even if the client company is a fresh start-up with no track record, you must create an image that says "this company is going to succeed."

Look again at the two logos above. The one on the left is typical of what I call "elementary school designs." You can see a lot of similar logos every year when newspapers let 12-year-old students enter "design-an-ad" contests. The logo on the right isn't world-class, but it certainly does convey a stronger image than the other one. Your first job as a logo designer is to make your client's business look successful. In order to do your job well, you're going to have to ask the client some questions. Every logo job *must* begin with questions. And when you do ask these questions, take notes. Write down things that you think are important. And after you have left your meeting with the client, review the notes. You may think of some other things that might be important to ask.

The size of the business and the complexity of its product mix will be a determining factor in what (and how many) questions are asked.

For the typical small business, the questions might be simple, such as:

1. What is the nature of the goods and services being sold?
2. What is the geographic reach of the company?
3. Who buys the goods and services (customer demographics)?
4. What changes are anticipated in the next few years?
   (areas such as product mix, expansion plans, locations, etc.)

The answers to these questions will give you a good start in planning your design parameters.

Questions to ask for larger projects.

When you do projects for larger firms (particularly manufacturers or large retailers/wholesalers) you will need to ask a lot more questions in order to get a grasp on the identity needs of larger companies. The following questions below give you some idea about the type questions you should ask the larger clients.

1. What is the company's history? Old firm or young? In same business all the time, or have changes been made?
2. Is the company part of another larger organization? If so, what is the relation to the larger firm's corporate identity?
3. Where does the company do business? Are there any other facilities in different locations? Are there sales reps covering different regions?
4. What does the company market? What is the primary advantage of the company's products over the competition? What are the drawbacks? Is the company a market leader or a follower?
5. What is the reputation of the company among its particular industry?
6. Why did the company decide to consider a new identity? Is this plan a response to a problem?
7. How does company management envision the future of the firm?

8. How will the product mix of the company change in the next five years? Will new technology have any impact on these plans?

9. What is the quality level of the company's products and services? Luxury? Discount? Somewhere in between?

10. What is the company's current corporate identity? (Ask to see samples of virtually everything with the company's logo.)

11. What image does management want the company to have five years from now?

This is not meant to be a complete listing, but it will certainly give you a starting point in the question process. The individual differences in various companies will lead you to different types of questions. Be alert for answers which will lead to new questions.

Gathering samples & photos.

After you have asked the client all the appropriate questions you can come up with, ask to see samples of virtually everything which carries the company logo. There will be the standard stationery items, and you'll likely discover more printed forms and other paper items than even the company realized it had. And you've just started.

Next, get a camera and take photos of all the company's signs, all its trucks, and all other applications that show a name or a logo. By the way, when I say **all** its trucks, and **all** its signs, that's what I mean. If you get only representative samples of each, you'll probably leave out some variation of the company name set in type and the logo.

What to expect from most companies.

You'll probably find that the company's existing corporate identity isn't anything near being consistent, and you'll likely find that there are many minor (or major) variations in the logo. The name will likely be set in many various styles of type, and in the company color will have a number of variations. (On one project I managed, the company color was listed as "blue," and the shades ranged from navy to a sky blue.)

This lack of consistency is due to the likely fact that the company never had a *planned* identity before. There may have been a standard logo at one time, but printers, sign painters and other crafts people are prone to change or slightly modify these designs for their own needs and reasons. The same goes for color and type. Printers may want to run your job right behind another that has a "blue" on the press. Never mind the fact that your blue is shades away from the one that will be run.

Equity.

When you study over all the samples of the company logo applications, you're looking for something that people in the identity business call "equity."

Equity in an existing corporate identity is something like equity in a house that you've lived in for a while. You've spent money on monthly payments, and as a result, you have built up some value over and above your mortgage balance. With a corporate identity, equity is developed through usage over the years. In the case of a visual identity, though, equity may be one or more of these items:

1. the colors
2. the type face
3. the basic design of the logo
4. one of the design elements in the logo
5. the basic shape of the logo

A logo may need to be changed for many reasons. Logos, like office equipment, will wear out over time. When a logo is outdated and is no longer a good marketing symbol for a company, it's time for a change. The logo design consultant must consider the equity of the old logo. Below is a case history of how Westinghouse Electric has changed its logo over the years. Notice how the circle (basic shape) and the "W" (design element) were retained in the changes.

17

Here's another example of how a company, John Deere, has maintained the equity of its previous logos in more than 100 years of changes.

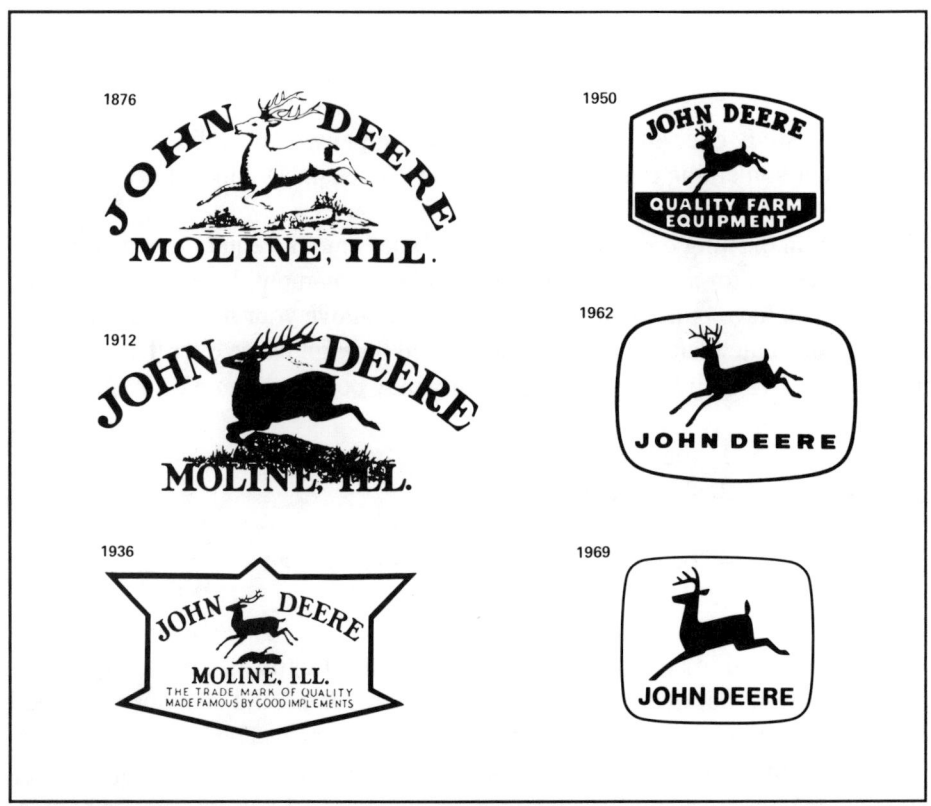

Equity: a summary.

When you are planning a new corporate identity for any client, you will need to look over samples of how their logo is being used. Among small firms, you'll likely find that there are a number of variations in the logo, type and color. In some cases, there will be some equity existing, even among all the inconsistency. If there is equity in a firm's identity, you need to build on it, as in the examples for John Deere and Westinghouse.

In some cases, though, there will be nothing of value worth carrying over into a new logo. In cases such as those, you need to break fresh ground and design a logo that will be an appropriate visual representative for your client.

Here are four different logos currently in use for a client. Is there equity worth carrying over into a new design? *Type:* probably not. *Logo:* three different variations make some use of a camera lens for the visual. Perhaps this could be adapted in a positive way. *Name:* what will the name be? What would you do with this project? This is a good practice exercise for beginning logo designers.

Jim Wilson Photography

19

Here are a number of logos being used on different items for an inexpensive men's shop. Needless to say, there's little here worth retaining in the new logo. The only element that is used consistently is the circle, but it's not necessary to maintain it in the new design

MB Mister Buster's

MB Mister Buster's

Mr B Mr. Buster's

MB Mister Buster's

MB Mister Buster's

Sometimes, a existing logo can be changed slightly and improved considerably. Here is an original logo which was beginning to show a little age.

With a minor modification to the logo, plus a change in the type, the logo has a new visual vitality.

Corporate identity checklist.

The following is a corporate identity checklist which I have used for a number of years. It will help you cover all the items needed in planning a corporate identity program.

Basic Identity

- Corporate Mark
- TradeMarks
- Trade Names
- Logotypes
- Signatures
- Corporate Colors
- _____
- _____

Advertising/Promotion

- Consumer Magazines
- Trade Magazines
- Newspaper
- Television
- Booklets
- Brochures
- Catalogs
- Direct Mail
- Posters
- Point of Purchase
- Premiums
- Giveaways
- Dealer Publications
- News Releases
- Corporate Periodicals
- Dealer Publications
- _____
- _____

Financial & Legal

- Annual Reports
- Quarterly Reports
- Proxy Statements
- Legal Documents
- Standard Contracts

Transportation

- Company Cars
- Trucks
- Truck Trailers
- Vans
- Aircraft
- Ships
- Freight Cars
- Tank Cars
- Material Handling Equipment
- _____
- _____

Exterior Signage

- Plant Entrance
- Office Entrance•Retail
- Outlets
- Directional Signage

Interior Signage

- Doors
- Directional Signage
- Plant Signage

Environmental Graphics

- Offices-Interiors
- Decor & Furniture

Stationery & Forms

- Letterheads, standard
- Letterheads, executive
- Letterheads, monarch
- Envelopes, standard
- Envelopes, executive
- Envelopes, monarch
- Envelopes, window
- Mail labels
- Large envelopes
- P.O. forms
- Invoices
- Proposals
- Reports
- Miscellaneous forms

Packaging

- Products
- Labels
- Price tags
- Stickers
- Cartons
- Boxes
- Bottles
- Cans
- Point-of-purchase

Miscellaneous

- Plant, external
- Office, external
- Machinery, external

Chapter 4
Setting Design Parameters

Once you have asked the client all the questions you had in mind, and after you have made a visual survey of the existing items using the client's corporate identity, you need to set design parameters. This is a written statement in which you write details of the graphic system that you intend to produce to meet the client's needs.

The design parameters statement can be as short as a paragraph, or it may involve several pages. In general, the larger the company (with more applications) the longer the design parameters statement.

Why make a written statement of your visual intentions? I find that it's a good way to make sure that I keep on track with my plan. It helps to read over the statement every day or so during a project, just to avoid chasing an idea that may not fit in with the client's needs.

In order to show you a sample design parameters statement, I have created a fictitious advertising agency called "Tri-Ad," whose existing logo is shown below.

During the questions part of the project, the client indicated that he felt the logo looked old fashioned and rather staid. He felt that the type was a little too ordinary for a creative business.

Unlike most firms, Tri-Ad did use the logo pretty consistently. There were no other designs in use, and the color was always the same.

The client's primary concern was summed up: "we're a lot better than our logo."

23

The design parameters statement.

Here's what we wrote:

The client's logo is a little outdated, primarily due to the very common use of three triangles stacked below the name set in type. While the type may not be outdated as much as the client thinks, the way it is *used* tends to make it look rather stodgy.

In creating a new logo, we will:
1. maintain the equity of the basic shape of the logo
2. maintain the equity of the 3 triangles. We will do a different configuration of the 3 elements, in order to give it a more modern twist. We believe that with the name being "Tri-Ad" the use of the 3 triangles may have some positive factors.
3. create a design which does not include type within the basic shape.
4. specify a type face that presents a somewhat modern feeling, yet one that has classic style, for long-term use.
5. do something with the type to emphasize the "ad."

The new logo.

Using those parameters, here's what we came up with. Check out all aspects of the design, and you'll see that we did everything we set out to accomplish. That's a major reason for having the design parameters statement.

24

Chapter 5
Good logo and bad logos

What makes a good logo? What makes a pretty woman? What makes an attractive building? How do you define *visual quality* by using words? In order to design a good logo, you should be able to recognize one when you see it.

Keep in mind that we're talking about a logo that not only looks good, but one that also serves as a communications and marketing tool for a company. So we aren't just talking about *pretty* here. A good logo for a beauty salon wouldn't work at all for a steel manufacturer. Without trying to further define "good logo," let's look at a list of characteristics that any logo should have. If you wish, you can use this as a check list to apply to any logo which you design.

1. *Appropriate for the business.* Does the design "look right" for the company who will use it? Does it convey the proper imagery? A design for a tire distributor and one for a jewelry store should have little in common. Whenever possible, the logo should graphically suggest something about the business. (For many firms, this is not possible, but when the product or service lends itself to this application, do it.

The logo at left would be better suited for a heavy industrial company.

25

2. *Appropriate for use in all media.* The logo should work equally well when used on a business card (in a very small size) or on a billboard (maybe several feet tall). This seems simple enough, but many logos become unreadable when they are reduced to less than an inch for use on a business card. Highly detailed designs simply won't work in small sizes. The logo below is good: at first glance. But then notice how it does not retail its clarity and boldness when it is reduced to business card size.

Also, if the logo is to be used on TV commercials, use of thin lines will create a visual distortion on a home television set, which has more than 500 "scan lines" that make up the picture. This effect is multiplied if the thin lines are on a diagonal plane.

Shape of the logo is also an important factor. A logo that is extremely tall or wide will not fit properly for most applications, and will either: a. take up too much space, or b. be too small to be effective. A good rule is to have everything fit comfortably into roughly a 2 x 3 to 2 x 5 ratio. Anything wider is going to give you headaches. It'll be a problem on items such as business cards, letterheads, signs, etc.

This is the maximum width ratio for a logo.

3. *Works equally well in black and white as in color.* The computer lets you do some terrific designs in multiple colors. But the reality is that most logos will be reproduced in black and white (or black plus one color) most of the time. Few businesses can afford to have all their printed material produced in full color. When you finish a logo that involved color, print it out in black and white to make sure that it communicates as a single-color design
The logos below all require color to be successful. Avoid doing designs like this.

4. *Simplicity works.* The highly complex logo has many drawbacks. It is hard to see when it is reproduced in a small size. Several competing images within a single small design may result in a muddled message. The point to remember here is: *when you try to say too much, you may end up saying nothing at all.*

The logo on the left is overly busy; there is not a single focal point of the design. The logo on the right has a lot of movement, yet it is strong and memorable, with a single enhanced element.

5. *Strong tonal contrast.* A design that is "washed out" or that blends into the paper will not be sufficiently strong to communicate the desired message. Use bold visuals whenever possible. Even "dainty" companies (such as cosmetics) must have a solid foundation for graphics. You can still get the desired soft effect with the right type face.

The logo on the left has thin lines and is a weak symbol. The logo on the right, which is essentially the same design, is strong, and bold. (Note how they reproduce in business card size below.)

6. *Appropriate type face.* The company name must be in a type face that sends an appropriate visual signal. Every font has certain characteristics: masculine/feminine, weak/strong, new/old, progressive/staid, etc. Choose your type with care. Also, "fad" type faces can "date" a logo as much as fins on automobiles date a car as being from the late 1950s. Avoid highly unusual type for corporate identity. Remember, this is long-term design. You're much safer when you stick with the classic fonts (or their newer descendents). The various type faces on the following page show just a few of the fonts available for your computer today. (You can buy nice 250 fonts for $50, and your first inclination is to want to use them all. Try to avoid the temptation on corporate identity projects.)

Some of the fonts here are highly usable for corporate identity purposes, while others will "date" the design, while others will be virtually timeless.

Times Bold

This face will never give away its age.

Windsor Bold

Windsor has already run its course, while Helvetica is always in style for corporate identity.

Helvetica Black

University Roman

These two fonts are nice for special applications, but they are too ornamental for corporate ID use.

American Typewriter

7. *Clarity of purpose.* Don't get too tricky with abstract visual devices which require the reader to spend time figuring out what you have in mind. (They won't do it.) Always remember that the logo design project is creating a corporate marketing tool for long-term use. Don't make this into your personal creative exercise to show how "arty" you can be.

The first "Louisa Supply" logo below says nothing about the business. The bottom one makes a statement about the nature of the company.

In order to get a feel for what makes a good logo, you might want to buy some of the many good books available about corporate identity.

Chapter 6
Selling and presenting your work.

How much do you charge for a logo?

You have probably read articles about logo changes made by major companies. The mention of a "million dollar fee" for the design firm has probably stuck in your mind. Of course, you'd like to get a project like that, wouldn't you?

Before you start shopping for the Mercedes and the beach-front condo, let's cover the issue of what your logo is worth to a company.

Those highly-publicized "million dollar fees" for design firms are the exception, and only a handful of major design organizations have the abilities to attract projects like that. In nearly all cases, the client who is *paying* that fee is a multinational corporation. Why would they pay that much — just for a logo?

The answer is that they're getting a whole lot more than a logo. The design firm that is getting that huge fee starts the project by doing research, *thousands of hours of research*, about the client, its customers, its perceptions, and many small details that are all considered before the next step is undertaken.

Next, a highly detailed design statement is done. This is a paper which merges the company's long-term marketing plans with its corporate identity needs. The result is a comprehensive "road map" that the design firm's staff will follow as it prepares rough concepts. In this statement, the "equity" of the current design is one of the many items which is explored in depth

Next, there may be hundreds — even thousands — of rough sketches done of a possible new logo. In this process, it is common for minor variations of the current logo to be produced. Sometimes, the "new logo" is actually a slight revision of the old one. During this process, the design firm may present some or all of these roughs for the client to review.

Once the client has narrowed down all the roughs into a group of "finalists," the design firm may once again do some time-consuming and expensive market research into the images provoked by the various designs. This testing may be done with consumers, prospects, employees, investors, and many other specific audiences.

Finally, once the new logo has been approved by the client's senior management, it is then applied to hundreds or thousands of applications from printed materials to signs to vehicles. The corporate identity manual showing all these applications may run to more than 300 pages. And the actual cost of actually making all these changes can be monumental. When you consider that thousands of trucks must be re-painted, all stationery, catalogs, etc. must be re-printed, and all other items carrying the logo are changed, you can see how the costs mount quickly. Many multinational firms have reported that the costs of implementing the new logo at over $10 million. It's no wonder that the client doesn't balk at a million dollar design fee — it's just 10% of the total cost of the project.

The items I've just mentioned are but a few of the details of the big, high-budget projects. Needless to say, if you just bought this book to learn how to do logos, you aren't likely to get one of these projects. The fact is, there are about a half-dozen corporate identity consulting firms in the world who are actually qualified to even bid for this size project. So, let's look at the lower end of the logo market, the place where you'll likely be able to compete.

So, how much can I charge for a logo?

You're probably going to be working for small clients, at least for a while. Your early clients will likely be local businesses, probably owned by one person. Your "contact person" will probably be the owner. Your fee is coming directly out of the owner's pocket, so he wants to feel he's getting his money's worth.

At this level, most people relate to a "per hour" billing system. This translates into "how many hours will you spend on my logo, and how long will it take you to do it?" You may already have a desktop publishing business in operation and may already have a "per hour" rate established, but in case you don't, the next few paragraphs will be of value to you.

Setting your hourly rate. You start by deciding how much you want to make per hour. (Be realistic. We'd all like to make $500 or more per hour, but we have to find a willing buyer.) Just for conversation's sake, let's assume you'd like to make $20.00 per hour, which comes out to about $40,000.00 per year. (Your goal right now may be lower or higher, but these numbers are easy to work with. Since I never was too good at math, we'll stick with the round numbers.)

If you want to have a gross pay of $20 per hour, you need to consider all the bills that you have to pay before you get *your* check. There's rent, the phone bill, your insurance, utilities, payroll (if you have employees), office supplies, new software, gasoline, etc. All those items have to be paid for from your income from projects. Also, add in some for "profit" to be stashed for future needs. Most sources indicate that your total overhead will be two to three times the amount of your personal income. So, if you want to make $20 per hour, you should charge anywhere from $60 to $80 per hour.

"My clients will never pay that much per hour," you might say. That's OK, because you probably won't sell the job on a per hour basis anyway. Most clients want to know "how much will the logo cost me?" They don't want to pay you extra if the job takes more hours than you had originally figured, so most jobs will be sold on a "flat fee" basis.

For most local clients, your job will actually consist of a new logo, plus stationery set. So, once the logo is approved, you'll produce an envelope, letterhead and card in camera-ready form.

How much to charge? When you're estimating the time the job will take, don't just include the time at your computer. Be sure to consider client meetings, travel time to get to those meetings, and time spent getting information about the project. With the power of the computer to let you work so quickly, you may spend only an hour or two actually at the screen. But when you consider the meetings (two seems to be a minimum number possible) and other time, you'll probably have at least 5 hours on a small logo project. If you allow a couple of extra hours for the average small project, then let's put down *7 hours* as the magic number for now. Let's split the $60 to $80 per hour figure from above and get $70 per hour. Multiply that by 7 hours and you get $490 for the whole project.

Now, you can round this number off to $500 for a logo design project, and tell the world "for 500 bucks, I'll do you a logo and stationery set." You may get a lot of jobs at that price, or you may discover that the local market for similar projects is $200, $300 or some other figure less than your desired $500. If that's the case, you'll have to either meet the market price, or be better than your competition if you want much work.

In order to sell logos, you'll most likely need to show your prospect some of your work for *other* clients. But what if you don't *have* other clients, and you're just starting? There are a couple of options here. One: work for free. Do a couple or three jobs for friends or family. For nothing. Then, you have something to show. Another option: do some sample projects for hypothetical clients. Show them to your first prospects and explain that you're just starting. Offer to do their job at highly reduced rate. (Anywhere from free to 50% of your desired price is "highly reduced.")

After you've done a few jobs, if your work is good at all, you'll probably begin to get referrals from "word of mouth." Eventually, you may get a job that requires more than just the logo and stationery set. That's when you need to change your price to reflect the amount of work you'll be doing. Frankly, when you get this first "step-up" job, I wouldn't be too concerned with getting every nickel possible from this larger client. Approach it as an opportunity for you to show what you can do with a bigger project. Charge a little less than you think you should get. If you do a good job, the client will be very happy, and this will lead to more of the larger jobs. Then, you'll have the experience of several similar projects so that you can estimate the number of hours the project will take.

Fee setting is not a science, but after several jobs, (or after *losing* several jobs because your quote was too high) you'll discover just what the market will bear in your particular area.

Presenting your work.

OK. You've spent some time interviewing the client to see his long-term needs, and you've spent a few hours at the computer and have some designs you think are really terrific. Now what? It's time to sell the client.

There are several different theories on how to present (and sell) your work to the client. I've developed my own way over several years of trial and error, and it works for me. Yet other designers have totally different approaches that work for them. I'll tell you some of the principles, and let you decide which is best for you.

When I make a client presentation, I have one rule: I never show the client a proposed logo that I don't think is good. (What if he *wants* it?) Clients can have some strange tastes, so whenever you show a proposed logo to a client , be prepared to have it seen all over town.

How I make presentations.

After the information gathering is over, I normally do anywhere from ten to fifty roughs on the Macintosh. From that group, I'll normally choose a half dozen as being good enough for the client to use. Nearly always, one will be ***the logo***. The one I like best will get special treatment. I may have it reproduced in its proposed color. I'll do a mock-up of a stationery set. I may do sample signs as well as truck applications. In short, I'll show the client how it's going to look when it's applied to various items.

I take all the best roughs, plus my favorite logo and its applications when I make my presentation. I normally do this sitting at a board table, with three to five people sitting in. (I prefer to make a one-to-one pitch, but this is rare. The clients normally want the work to be seen by a core of top people.) I don't use easels of big presentation pieces. I begin by talking about the design parameters of the project. I may even pass out sheets to discuss why I took the directions I did. (See Chapter 15.) I then show them the roughs that I did "on the way to my final solution." I emphasize that these pieces were stepping stones to my best work. Finally, I show the favorite logo, as well as its applications. All my work is on typing size paper, so the people can touch and feel.

About 75% of the time, the client accepts my recommendation and adopts the logo I chose. Twenty percent of the time, they gravitate to one of the roughs I did "on the way." The other 5%, I have to go back to the screen and do some more work to show later.

Some designers will present only one logo. They'll sell it as hard as they can and hope that the client likes it. I've tried this. The drawbacks are (1) if the client doesn't like it and wants to see more, you leave him empty-handed for a while. (2) it's hard to come back and sell another logo equally hard when you've made such a strong pitch for your first one. (3) clients seem to think you've earned your fee more if you show that you did a lot of work on the way to your final solution.

You'll have to decide for yourself which way to present work. After a while, you'll probably come up with a method which is just right for you.

Chapter 7
Logo Design: Computer Style

If you're new to using computers for graphic design, you'll soon discover that it's very much like using a drawing board. However, there are some differences. Just for example, let's say you have a simple design in your mind that looks something like this:

If you plan to do this on the drawing board, you'll probably start by doing a circle. Nothing inside. Just a plain circle, like the one below.

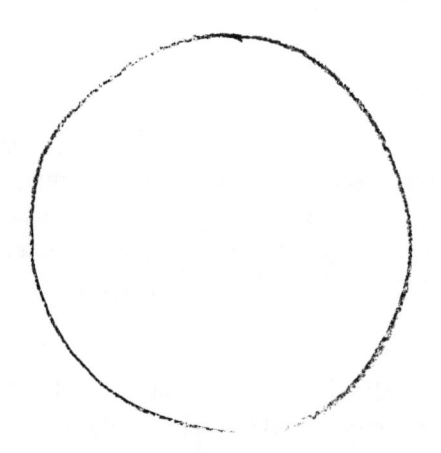

On the drawing board, your next step would be to draw lines to define where the white stripes will be, like this.

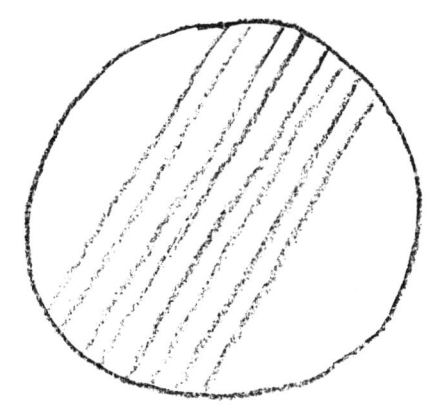

And finally, you'd fill in the circle. Your result is a rough sketch something like this.

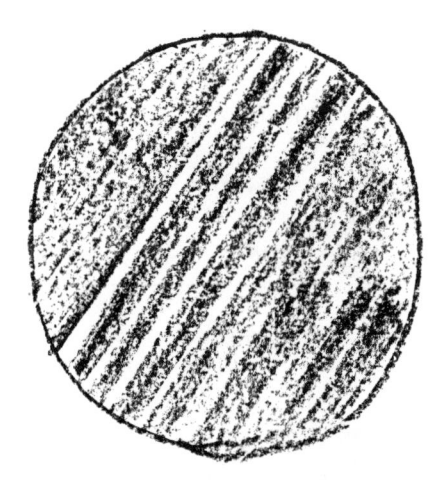

On the computer, you'll do it a little differently, and your result will be a much more advanced finished piece. Actually, on the computer, there's almost no such thing as a "rough sketch." Nearly all your computer graphic work can be considered to be "finished."

To get this same logo on the computer, you'll also start with a circle. However, your circle will be totally black. To get the desired white space in the circle, you'll put white design elements down on top of the black circle. It's a very simple and effective way to create graphics. You have to change your way of thinking just a little from the days B.C. (Before Computers).

Here's how you'd complete the same design: start with a circle (all black).

Add one diagonal white stripe.

Clone (copy) the stripe and move it to your desired position.

Duplicate the clone and move two times, and you have the finished design. The graphic above is actually complete, while the one you'd do with a pencil and paper is, at best, a rough. You'd still have to spend some time on it to make it into a finished piece. That's just one of the advantages of using the computer for graphic design.

Thinking in terms of computer design.

Most people who have had some formal training in graphic design have learned to "think visually." This essentially means that the person sees the design in his mind and conceptualizes the way it's going to be produced on paper.

I've recently worked with several students who are new to computer graphics. Their typical first instinct is to want to use the computer mouse as a pencil, and the screen as paper. They haven't yet learned to transfer their visual thinking to computer terms. For example, they don't initially think in terms of using a white line on top of a black circle.

In order for you to learn to think in terms of computer logo graphics, you need to learn only two terms: base objects and graphic effects.

Base objects.

Every logo begins with a base object. It may be a circle, a rectangle, a letter, an abstract shape, a water drop, or some similar foundation. A number of base objects are shown below.

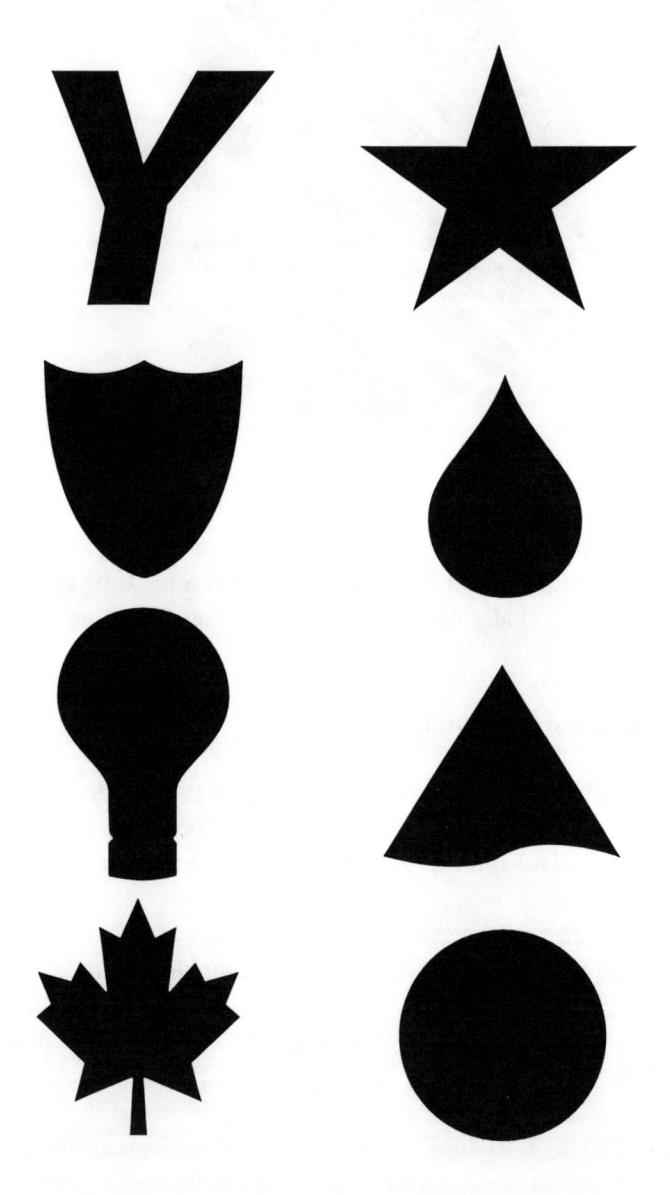

These base objects must be viewed as starting points for logos. It is only when something is added that they become complete designs.

Graphic effects.

Once the base object is in place on the screen, you modify it with one or more white (or light colored) graphic effects. The effects may be abstracts, stripes, a letter, a wave, or any other shape which will turn the base object into a logo. Each of the base objects from the previous page is shown below — with graphic effects added. This is logo design, computer style.

43

One of the major advantages of using the computer for design is that changes can be done very quickly and precisely. Let's take the design below, which was created just for this exercise. It's a nice look, but what if you (or your client) wants to see other options?

On the drawing board, it would take a while to make revisions in camera-ready form. But on the computer, you can make this change in a minute or so.

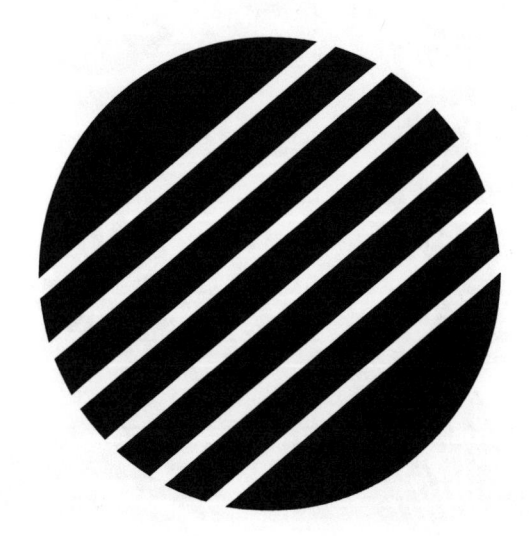

Similarly, you can make all these variations to the original design in just a minute or so on the computer. These designs show just a small sample of how the computer gives you a new set of tools for creating logos.

Chapter 8
Using Type Effectively

I remember well (1980) when my business bought a Compugraphic® typesetting system. The machine itself cost about $13,000 and the additional type we bought cost us about $12,000. The type was on very fragile filmstrips, and we got nearly 200 fonts for our twelve grand. We thought we were on the cutting edge of corporate graphics with all those different type faces.

Today, our old Compugraphic 7400 has gone on to a better life (gathering dust somewhere) and we have a Macintosh system that gives us more fonts than we can possibly imagine (or use!). I read an ad recently that offered 3,600 fonts for my computer for about $900. And just last week, I ordered a font package with 250 fonts (very nice ones, by the way) for $49.95. That's *20 cents per font*. With our old Compugraphic, we paid $60 per font!

The point of all this is that you now have access (cheaply) to literally thousands of fonts for your computer. And with all the visual manipulations that you can do with type, you have an infinite number of variations you can create from these inexpensive fonts. I guess the words here are: **be careful**. Just because you have access to all those fonts (and type tricks), that doesn't necessarily mean that all of them are good for use in corporate identity. After all, we're talking *long-term* design here.

Don't use overly ornate types. Don't do visual tricks that will quickly become cliches. Don't show how arty you can be with type.

Do remember that the type you select will be used with the logo for a very long time. You don't have to stay only with the classic fonts such as the Helvetica and Times families; there are many variations available today that will certainly remain in fashion for a number of years.

When you're looking at a type for possible corporate identity use, if you say to yourself, "wow, that's really an unusual font," don't use it. For corporate identity use, the best rule for type is: play it safe.

Serpantine Bold

1. **LogoType**

2. **LogoType**

3. ***LogoType***

4. **LogoType**

5. **LogoType**

6. **LogoType**

7. **LogoType**

With your computer's drawing program, you have access to a large variety of tools which let you modify the type in a number of ways. On the opposite page is a small sampler of some of the techniques you can use to change the appearance of type.

Note that every line shown was set in the same size of a font called Serpentine Bold. All the changes were made using tools within Aldus FreeHand.

1. The first line was set in FreeHand with no changes.

2. This condensed version of the type was done simply by tightening up on the letter spacing.

3. This type face does not have an italic version. To get this slant, I simply set it in FreeHand, then skewed it to the desired angle.

4. To get the overlapping letters, I simply converted the type into art, so that each letter was a separate element. Then, I changed each letter's border line to white. Finally, I overlapped the letters while keeping them all on the same horizontal plane.

4. Notice that this type is the same exact height as the original number one. To get the condensed version, I simply used the FreeHand pointer to change the "box" and make it narrower.

6. Getting the graduated shaded effect was as simple as converting the line to art, then using the "graduated shading" command in FreeHand.

7. This design involved converting the type to art, then separating the "L" and "T" from the line, enlarging the two letters, and placing them into position.

These are but a few of the things you can do with type. The main thing to remember about the sample on the other page is: when you look at a type sample, remember that it can be transformed into a number of other shapes and styles.

49

The three samples below give you some idea about how you can change letters significantly once you convert the type into art. This step gives you access to all the "design points" of each letter, and you can then make any change you can imagine. (The original type is on top, with no changes.)

When you want to create a name in type, yet give it a distinctive flair, consider using this technique.

Maxam

Maxam

Maxam

Here are a few other things to keep in mind about type used in a corporate identity project.

1. The type and logo are most often used together. They should be in a size where they complement each other. Don't let one dominate the other.

The top logo is too big for the type.

This type overwhelms the small logo.

This is a better size relationship between logo and name.

2. When you use a bold font for the corporate name (as above), don't use it in small sizes, such as with the address on stationery., The example at left shows problems that arise. The example at right is much better.

Name Corp.
100 Pearman Blvd.
Bellefonte, NY 11779

Name Corp.
100 Pearman Blvd.
Bellefonte, NY 11779

3. When designing letterheads, don't mix more than two fonts at a time. And don't use multiple variations of the same font. The top two examples show the confused visual that results when you try to mix too many fonts.

The bottom example shows the best way to make the company name stand out on a letterhead stack. The name is set in 12 point Helvetica Bold Condensed, while the rest of the address is in 11 point Helvetica Condensed.

The Clarke Corporation
3006 Indian Run Road
Flatwoods, Kentucky 41139

The Clarke Corporation
3006 Indian Run Road
Flatwoods, Kentucky 41139

The Clarke Corporation
3006 Indian Run Road
Flatwoods, Kentucky 41139

Chapter 9
Using Lines, Shapes & Color

Lines.

When you use a drawing pencil (or even a Rapidograph) you have only a small variety of lines available to you. With the drawing tools of the computer, you can specify the size of all your lines (in point sizes).

All the elements here are actually lines made by the computer. They range in size from 4 points at top to 144 points at the bottom.

53

Most drawing programs have a feature which allows you to specify arrow points as well as the end device. These are not obvious on most of the programs and it's easy to forget they exist. When it's appropriate to use this type graphic, remember how easy it is to create arrows.

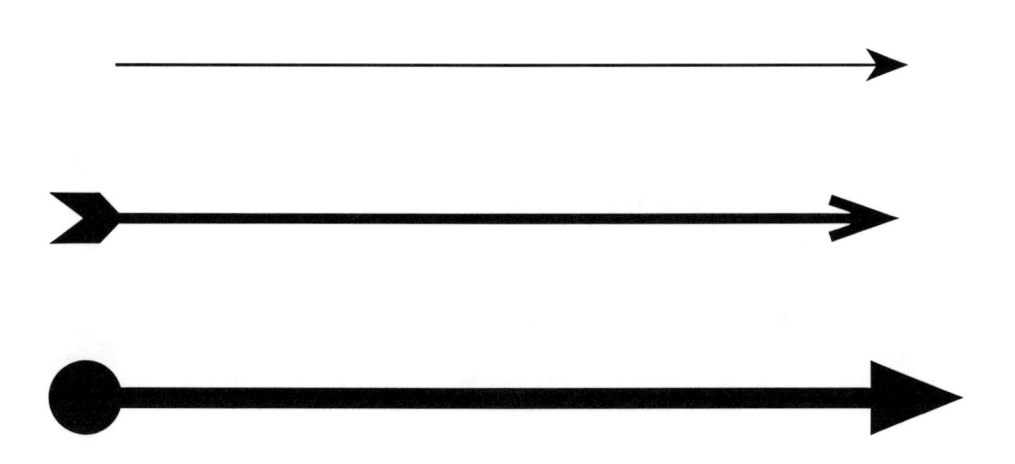

Shapes.

With all the drawing tools, you can create just about any shape you can imagine. You've already read about circles, ovals, squares, rectangles, etc. There's one feature on most drawing programs that gives you a whole array of shapes you can make which might have an application for corporate identity.

I call the shape the "round-cornered rectangle," Whatever you call it, you can specify the corner radius of the shapes. That gives you a great degree of flexibility in creating a base object. A few different samples of this shape are shown on the opposite page.

These four shapes were all done by changing the "corner radius" specifications on Freehand's tool that lets you draw round-cornered squares.

The top one has a degree radius setting of 14, The others have settings of (going down the page) 30, 45 and 60.

Color.

There are a few rules to keep in mind for using color in a corporate identity program.

1. Do not use more than two colors. Few firms can afford to have all their stationery, etc., printed in more than two colors.

2. Chose bold colors (not pastel) unless you're trying to create a very soft, feminine image.

3. Specify exact colors. Don't say "the corporate color is blue." There are about a hundred shades of blue. Don't take chances on printers getting the exact color you want. Choose a corporate color from one of the books with chips which specify exact shades of inks available. Specify that exact color for all jobs involving the corporate identity.

4. When you use two colors in your identity program, make sure they are compatible. (Don't use red and pink, for example).

5. On letterheads, type works best in darker colors, such as black, dark grey, dark blue, etc. Don't use light blue, light pastels, etc. Those colors will be hard to reproduce on photocopy machines and faxes.

6. Remember that you can get the effect of two colors by using a dark solid color on some parts of the printed piece, and screening the color for lighter use on other parts.

Chapter 10
Designing a Stationery System

Once you have completed a logo for a client, the next natural step is to design a stationery set: letterhead, envelope and card.

Friendly warning: A good logo can be screwed up by having a bad stationery set design. This chapter will give you some fundamentals for creating well-designed letterheads, envelopes and cards.

Note that this chapter title uses the words "stationery *system*." By "system," I mean a coordinated design, so that all the pieces in the set look as though they belong to the family It's all part of the Design Commandment: *"Be Consistent."* The design system you apply to your letterhead, envelope and card will also be used for paper items such as invoices, statements, mailing labels, fax cover sheets, etc. More about the need for consistent design system in a page or two. For now, though, let's look at the basics of beginning the design process on the stationery system. (I'm assuming that the logo is already completed and approved.)

To begin, I suggest you open a fresh page in your drawing program. For page size, choose 8.5 x 11 inches, the standard letterhead size in the US. (If you're doing a stationery set for an international client, check for the correct proportions.)

When the screen comes up, you then add a box to represent the left side of an envelope (make the box 4.125 inches deep, and about 5 inches wide.) Finally make a box to represent a full business card (3.5 wide x 2 inches deep.)

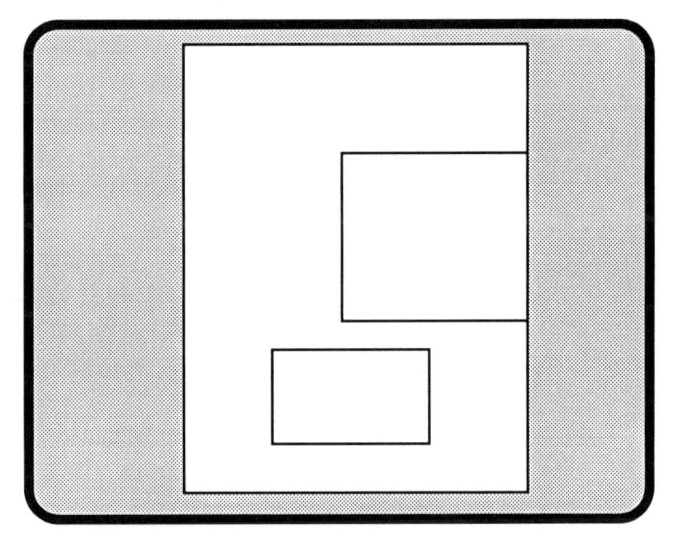

The completed screen should look something like this.

57

Controlled space.

Airplane pilots know that their navigation maps have areas labeled "controlled space." That means "don't get in this area, because you'll have some big problems." (such as a stray air force jet flown by a student pilot bearing down on you at 1,400 miles an hour.) Stationery design also has controlled space, but the results aren't quite so traumatic.

"Controlled space" on stationery items refers to areas which are reserved for other uses (such as typewritten matter on letters and envelopes, and postage and postal routing information on envelopes.) The "controlled space" areas for a standard letterhead set are shown here.

Unlike other stationery pieces, the business card will be used exactly as it is printed. So, in theory at least, there is no "Controlled space" on a card. You can use all of it for design if you wish. However, keep in mind that the card design should share a consistent look with the rest of the pieces.

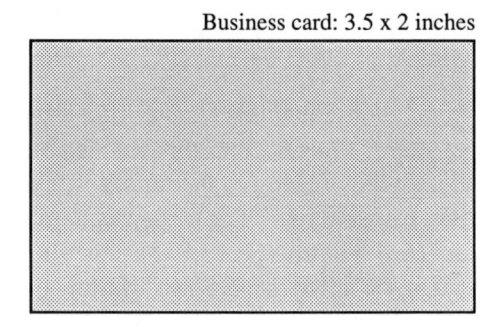

Business card: 3.5 x 2 inches

Business envelope: 3.5 x 2 inches

Envelopes have a typed address, a stamp (or meter imprint) and a place for postal routing codes. Not to mention margins needed by printers. You're limited to using the white space here. Everything else is controlled space.

Letterheads are to be typed on. It's amazing how many "designers" seem to forget this basic principle. The typing area should be totally free of any design elements whatsoever. Avoid using "screened" designs that take up large amounts of space. They only make communications more difficult. You can use the rest of the letterhead, including "bleeding" off the edge, but that costs more, so try to contain your design to the white area shown here.

Letterhead: 8.5 x 11 inches

Typing area.
Don't put any
design elements here.

Type.

Before you start to design your stationery set, let's cover the information that is going to be set in type.

1. Company name
2. Street address (or P.O. Box)
3. City, State, Zip
4. Phone (and Fax, too!)
5. Slogan or other tag line (optional)

All the above items will go on the letterhead. The envelope will also include all those items, except maybe the phone number. I say maybe because some firms have started to include the phone number on envelopes. Their theory is that the envelope might be the only item someone has handy, and why make that person call directory assistance to make a call. How do I feel about this concept? My corporate identity consulting business has the phone number on the envelope. (I want to make it as easy as possible for prospects to call me.)

Now for the card. It should have all the above information, and in addition should include the following:

6. Name of person
7. Person's title

Some business cards include other information such as

a. Factory address and phones
b. Product roster
c. Additional phone numbers of person

All this is OK, but it can be carried to extremes. The other day, someone showed me a card which included all these phone numbers (really):

Office phone: 555-1010
Home phone: 555-8787
Office fax: 555-9090
Home Fax: 555-9191
Car phone: 555-8765
Farm phone: 555-6364
Beeper pager: 555-1817

The guy was a stock broker. What else? He didn't want to miss even *one* call.

More type: some rules.

1. Don't use type that is too large. Since different type faces have different actual sizes, there is no hard rule on the maximum size. A 10 point type in one face can actually appear larger than a 9 point type in another font. (See the examples in the next paragraph. All the type is 11 point.) However, a good guideline is: don't use type over 11 points on a stationery set.

2, Don't use a fad type face or an overly ornate font on your stationery. The whole purpose of this thing is to *communicate.* Remember? You can never go wrong using type from the families of **Helvetica**, Univers, Times, Century, **Bookman, Garamond** or Goudy.

3. Use some contrast in the type faces to emphasize more important elements. This sample business card shows how bold face type is used for the company name and the name of the person.

Robert D. Smith
Director

Hooperman Company
703 Mantz Street
Burbank, CA 91523

(818) 555-9999 Fax: 555-9909

4. Use no more than two type variations within any one identity system. The variations above are: 1. bold type, 2. normal type. Other variations might be: 1. normal type 2. italic type. Or 1. Times Bold with 2. Helvetica. Both are shown below. If you go to more than two variations, you'll create visual confusion (and risk a citation from the design police.)

Hooperman Company
703 Mantz Street
Burbank, CA 91523

Hooperman Company
703 Mantz Street
Burbank, CA 91523

You could really screw up nice designs like this by having an additional variation such as the last line of the right example with italic type. Don't do it.

OK, enough fundamentals. Let's design a letterhead set. And do it with a consistent look. I wouldn't normally start with a card design, but since we have one on the previous page, let's use it and create a complete stationery set for Hooperman Company. (Note that the card is actual size here. Envelope and letterhead are reduced.)

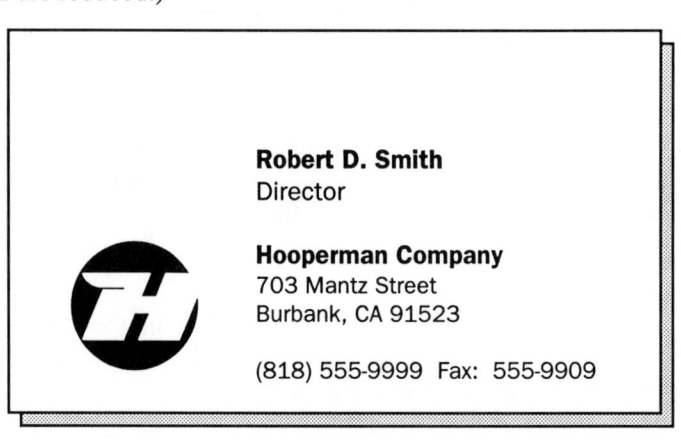

Robert D. Smith
Director

Hooperman Company
703 Mantz Street
Burbank, CA 91523

(818) 555-9999 Fax: 555-9909

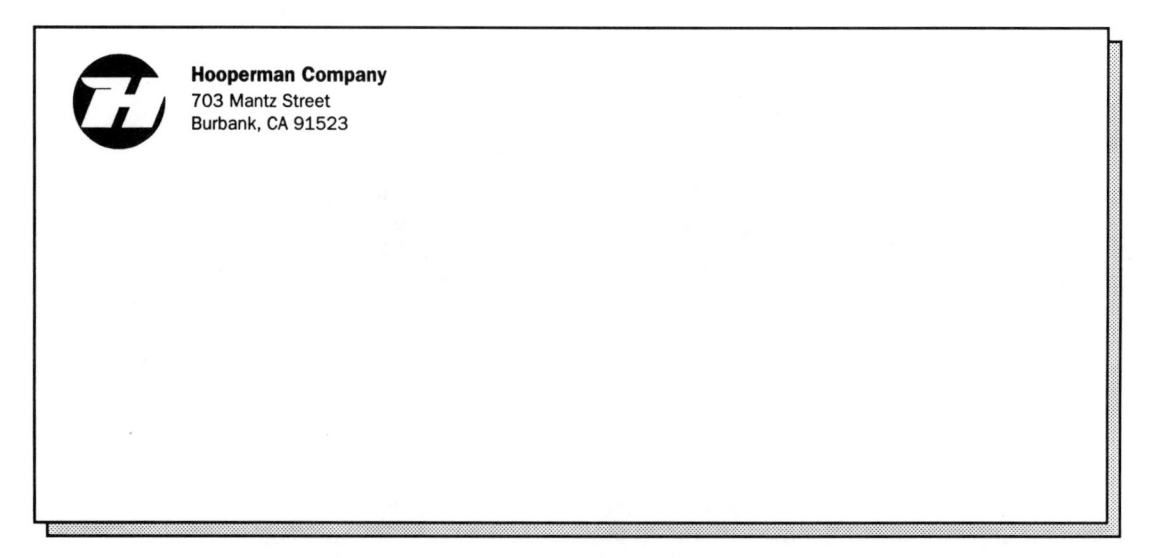

Hooperman Company
703 Mantz Street
Burbank, CA 91523

The type and logo on the envelope are smaller than they are on the letterhead. This is often done to allow for the difference of size between envelopes and letterheads. In addition, since the phone number does not appear on the envelope, the size relationship of the logo and the block of type has changed. **Note concerning letterheads:** many companies have a "second sheet" which is used for letters longer than one page. It normally has only the logo (and no type.)

Compare this letterhead design with the business card on the left page. (Remember that this letterhead is not shown full size.) The size relationship between the logo and the type has remained the same. And the position of the block of type is placed so that the left margin actually serves as an alignment guide for the typist.

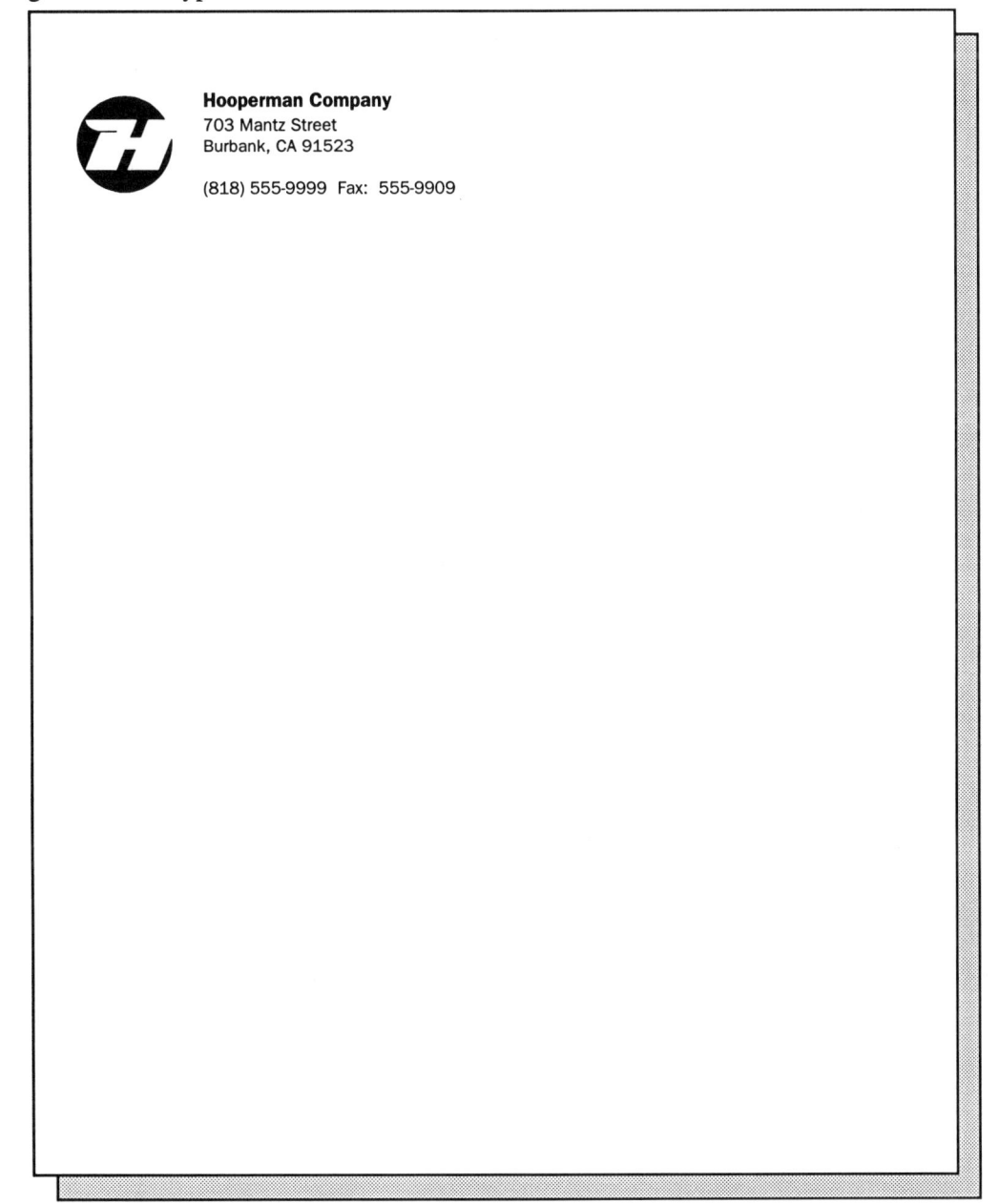

Hooperman Company
703 Mantz Street
Burbank, CA 91523

(818) 555-9999 Fax: 555-9909

Consistency: the wrong way.

The design system on the last page is planned so that everything hangs together, so that all the pieces look like they're part of the same family. Just by changing various elements a little and changing their relationships to each other, you can easily create a set of three pieces that have no family look. Kids: don't try this at home.

Hooperman Company
703 Mantz Street
Burbank, CA 91523

Robert D. Smith
Director

Hooperman Company
703 Mantz Street
Burbank, CA 91523

(818) 555-9999 Fax: 555-9909

All three pieces here use the same type face and the same logo, but their positions and various spatial relationships changed enough to destroy the consistency that is important to a design *system*.

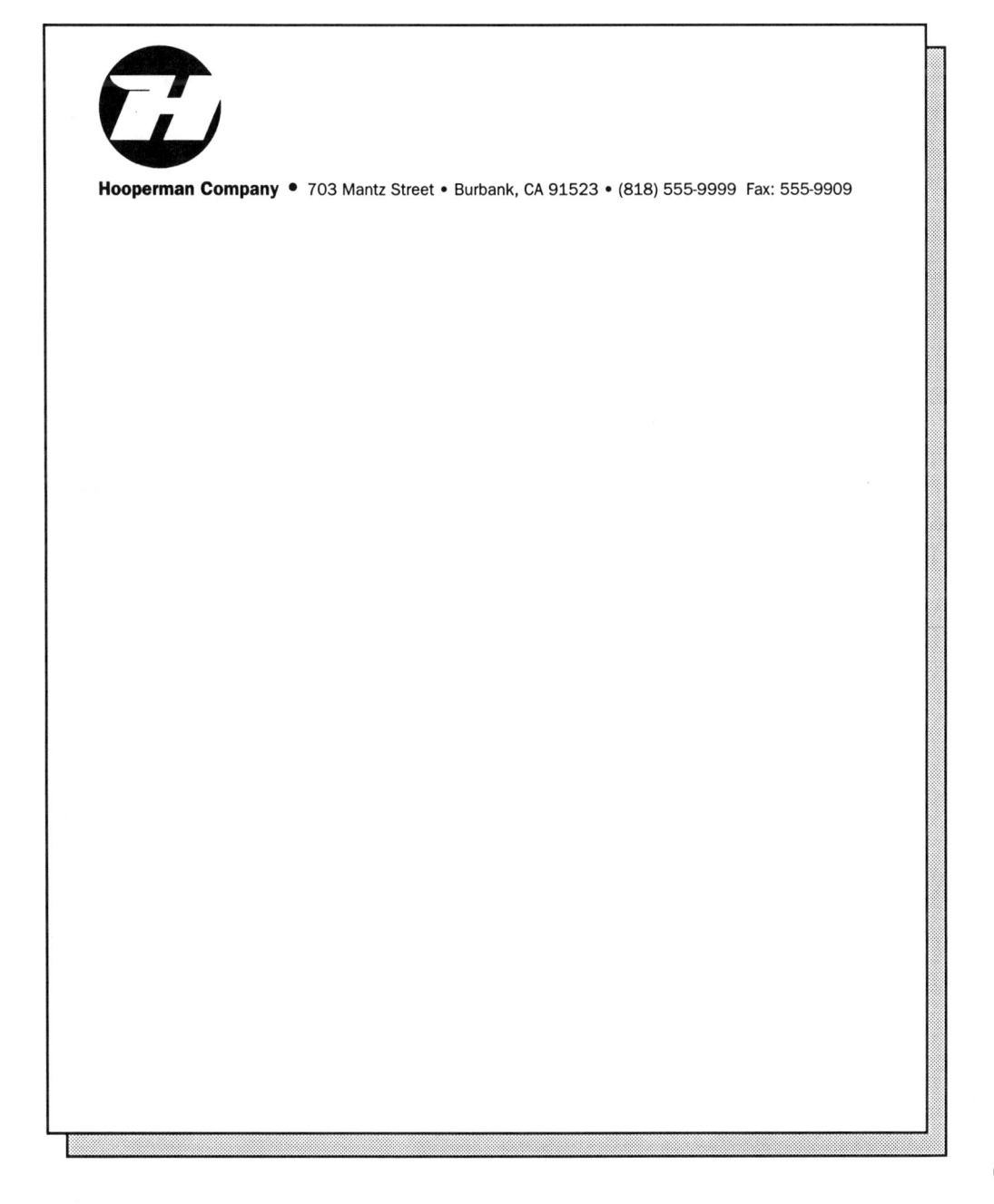

Check list for stationery systems:

This will help you to plan and execute stationery systems

- standard 8.5 x 11 inches letterhead
- executive 8.5 x 11 inches letterhead
- monarch size 7.25 x 10.5 inches letterhead (personalized)
- No. 10 standard envelope
- No., 10 executive envelope
- standard business cards
- executive business cards
- No. 10 window envelopes (for checks & invoices)
- 9 x 12 mailing envelopes
- mailing labels for large envelopes & parcels

You may also encounter firms with additional sizes of envelopes and other stationery needs. When you do a visual survey of the existing paper items, look for these extra items.

Chapter 11
Corporate ID Programs

Most of your early jobs will include only stationery applications. But one day, if your work is well accepted by clients, you're going to do a logo for a larger company which will require you to apply the logo to a large number of items beyond just letterheads, envelopes and cards.

This isn't especially difficult, but you do need to know some of the potential uses of the logo, as well as some of the guidelines to be used for such applications.

(Note: When the client company is sufficiently large, you'll need to prepare a "corporate identity manual," which is a set of graphic rules for the company. However, by the time you get a project that will be this large, you'll probably have a design library which will include a book or two about this subject. Frankly, it's too big a topic to tackle in a book like this.)

Anyway, this chapter is going to show you some sample applications, for a hypothetical client with a large variety of items which will include the logo.

In planning this particular project, we have set up a logo which is sometimes used *without* the company name set in type. This "logo only" use is often confined to applications that are totally internal, such as memos, warehouse fork lifts, etc. The samples in the following pages should give you a good idea on how decisions are made in projects such as this.

For the sales staff's cars, the logo is predominant, and it is important that the name also be bold. Note that it was not possible to use the same layout style for the car as was done for the stationery set in the previous chapter. In order to confine the logo and name to the front door, the elements were made put on different lines so that they would have high visibility.

This horizontal layout will fit well on items such as give-away pens, pencils, and other elongated pieces.

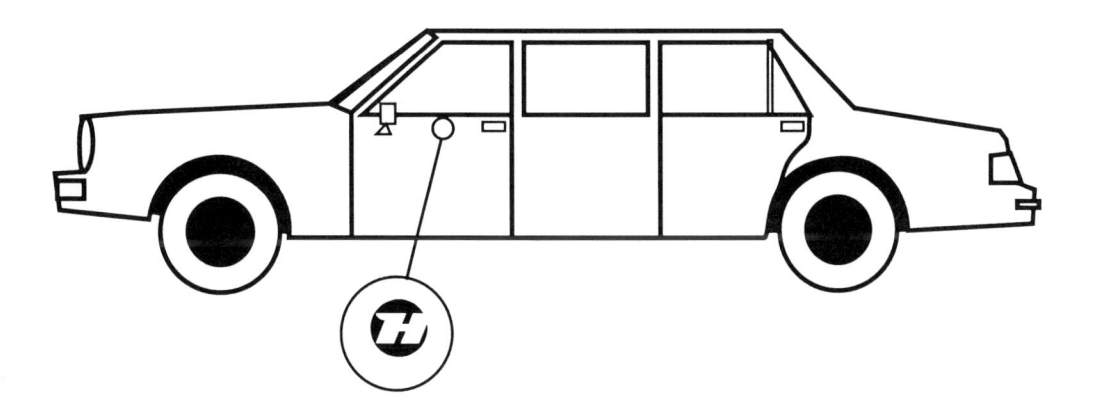

To create a feeling of "subdued class," the logo on the stretch limo will be very small and will not have the name. For company aircraft, the logo will be used alone — primarily due to space limitations

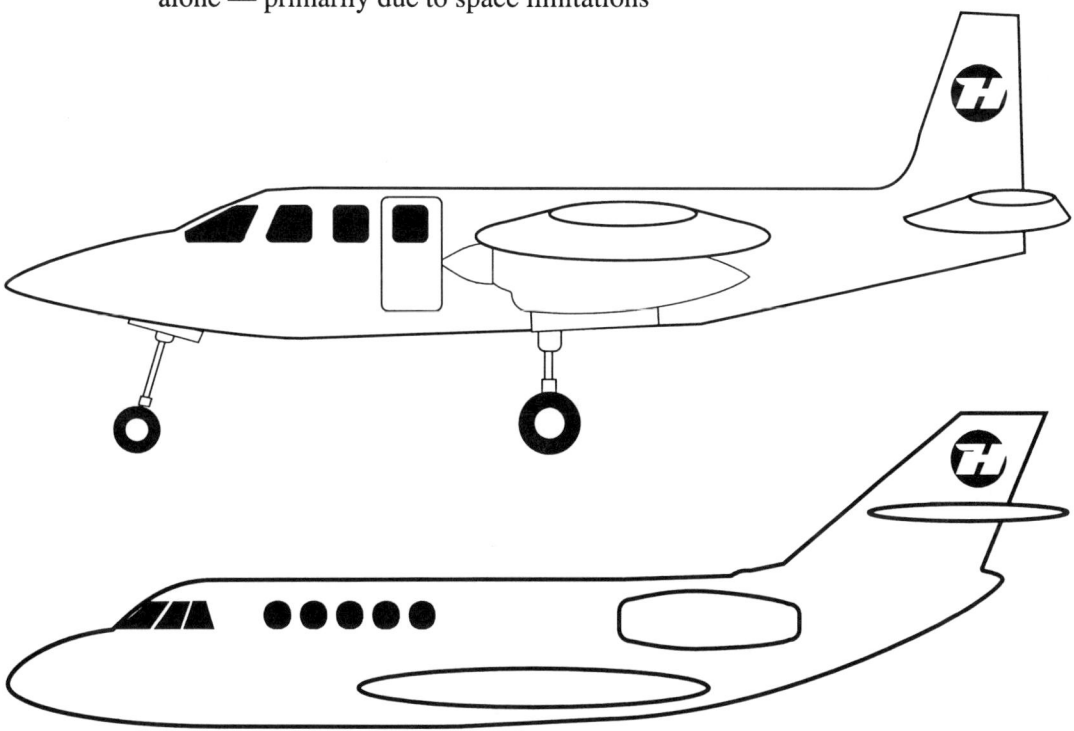

69

For doors inside the company's own buildings, the name and logo may be omitted. Directional information should be included. However, for space rented in other buildings, the name and logo should both normally be used, along with departmental information.

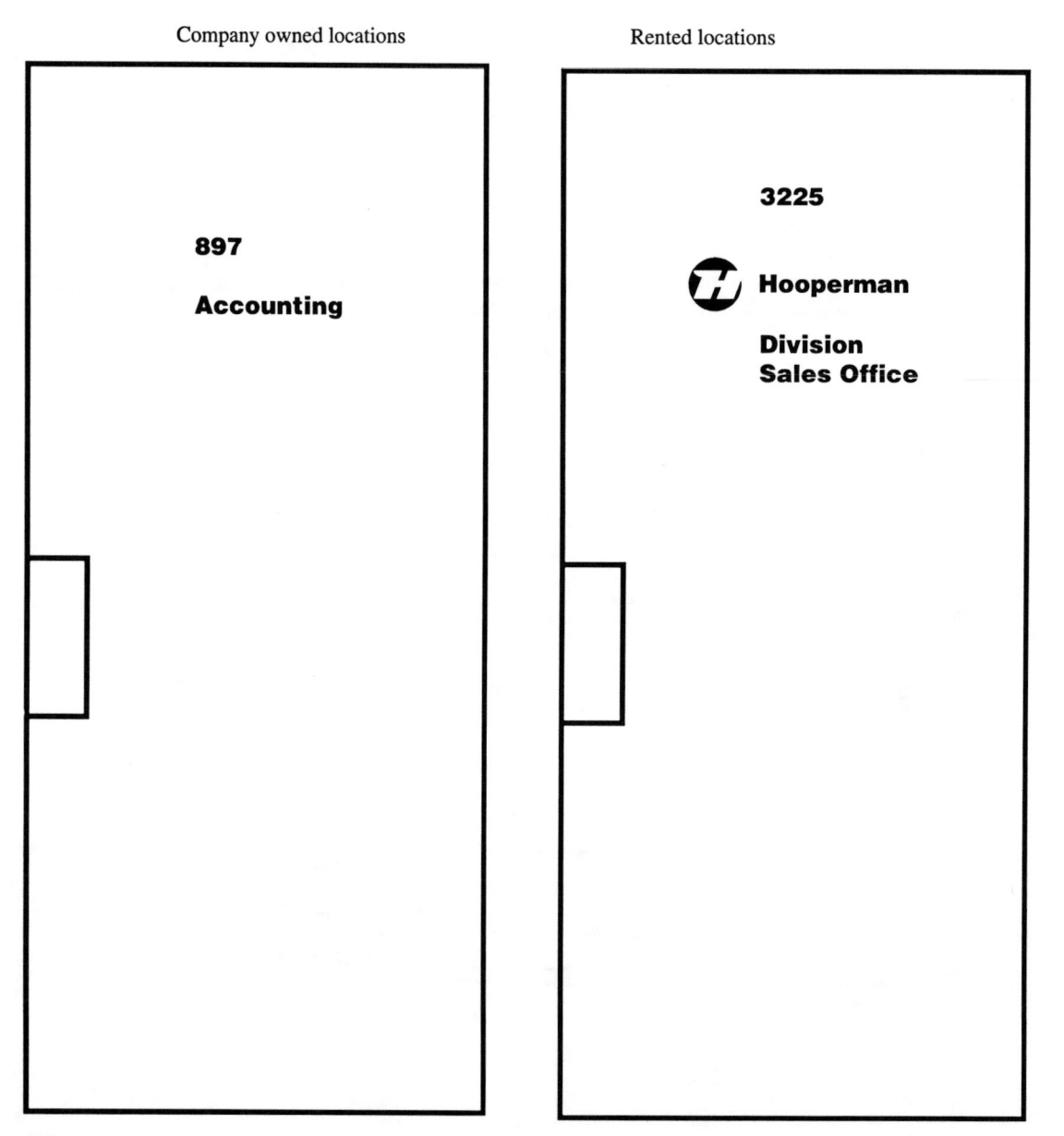

Company owned locations

897

Accounting

Rented locations

3225

Hooperman

**Division
Sales Office**

Mugs and other give-away items should include both the logo and name. However, plates, glasses and items used in the company dining rooms should have the logo only.

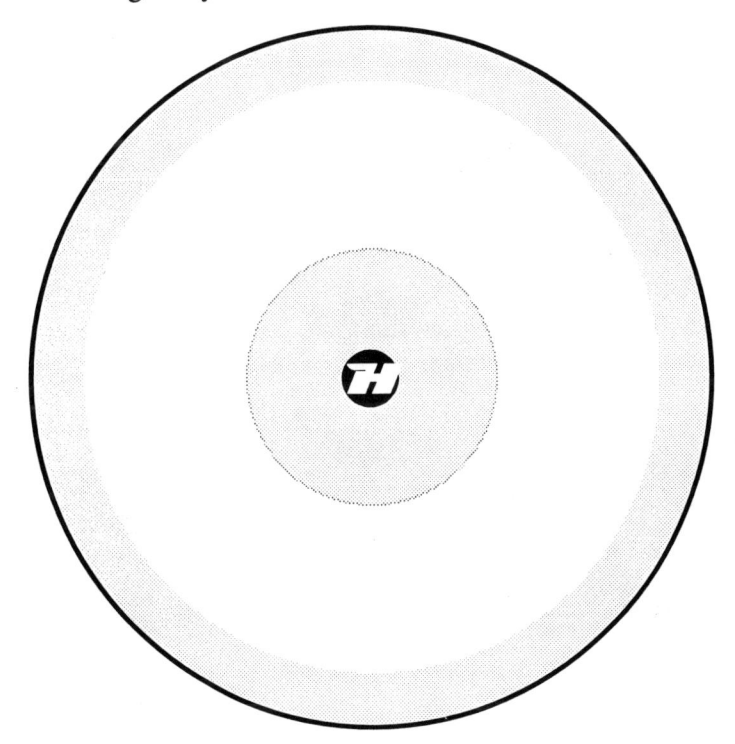

Computer mouse pads like the one above can use the preferred position of logo at the left of the name. However, for use on TV commercials, this would make the name and logo very small. The solution is to stack the logo over name as seen here.

72

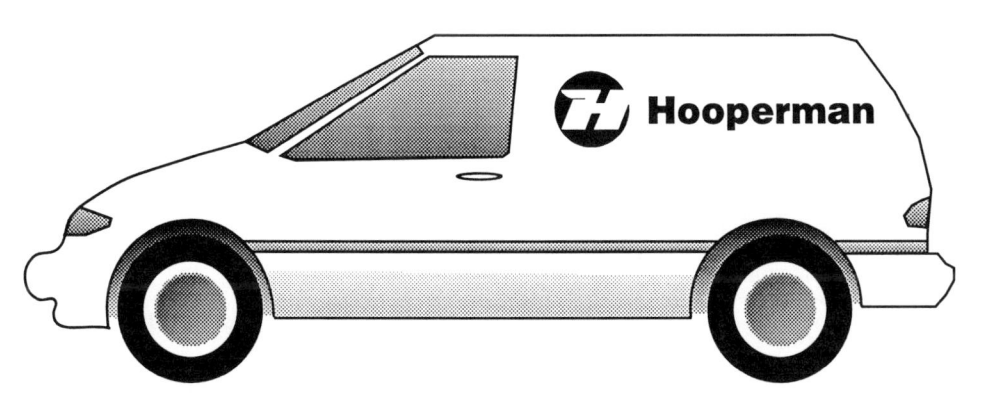

It is preferred to have the logo at the left of the name, as shown on this van and on the tanker rail car below. In the bottom example, the physical structure of the rail car would get in the way of letters and logo on a long horizontal line. The solution is to use the large middle panel and change the relative positions of the name and logo.

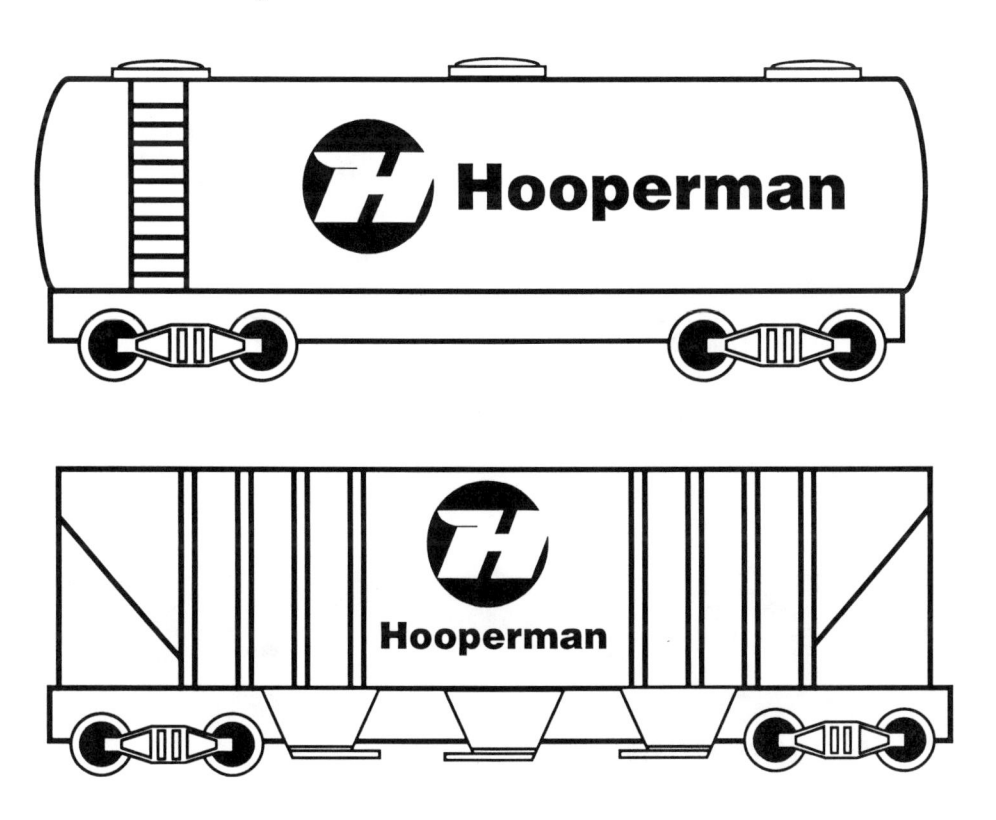

73

The hard hat and the uniforms will be worn by employees who work away from the company's primary locations. As a result, the logo and name will appear on various items of clothing.

For the blazer at right, the logo along will be used. Note: even though sales people will be wearing these at trade shows, etc., the name will not be included, in order to present the "subdued class" image that the company desires.

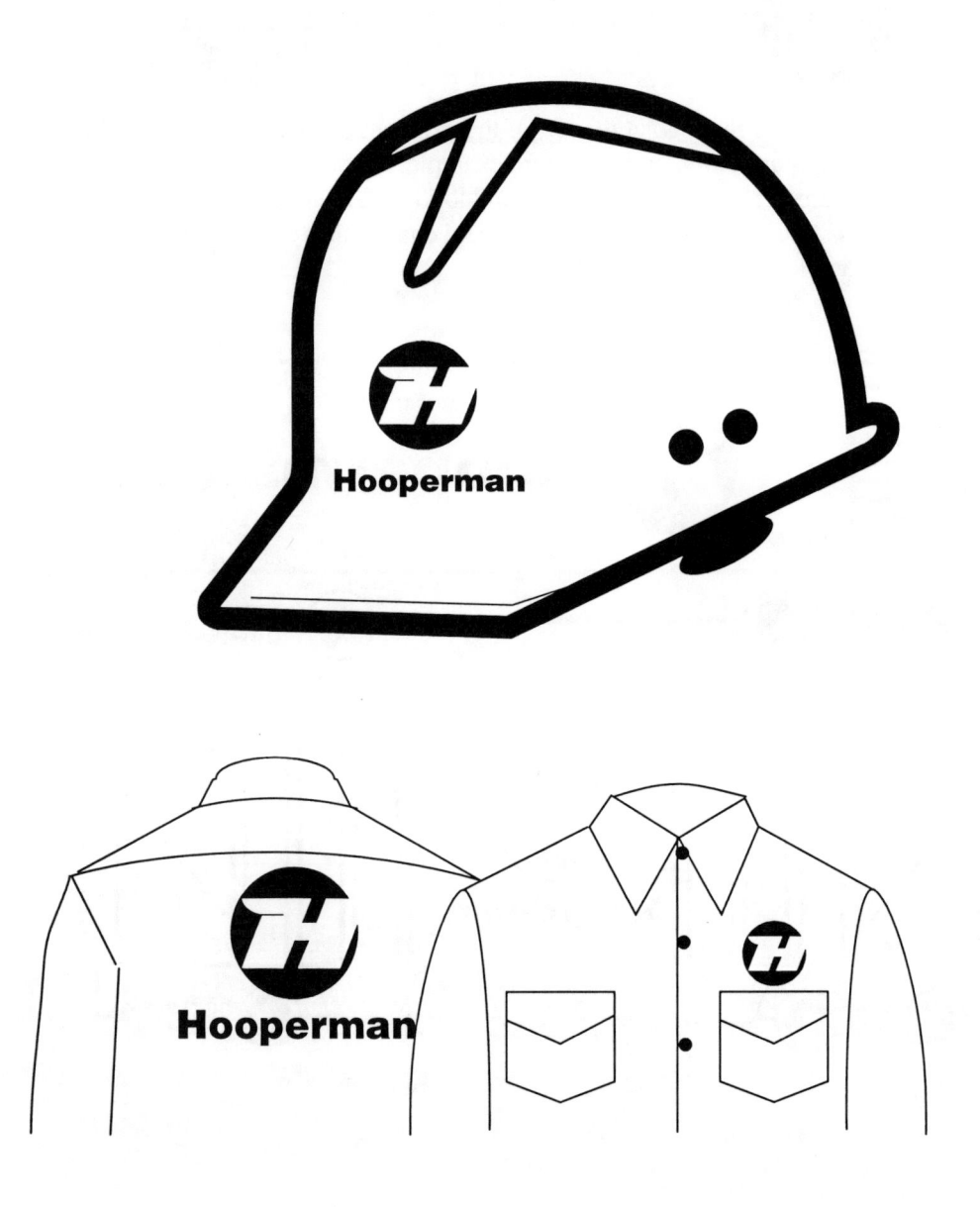

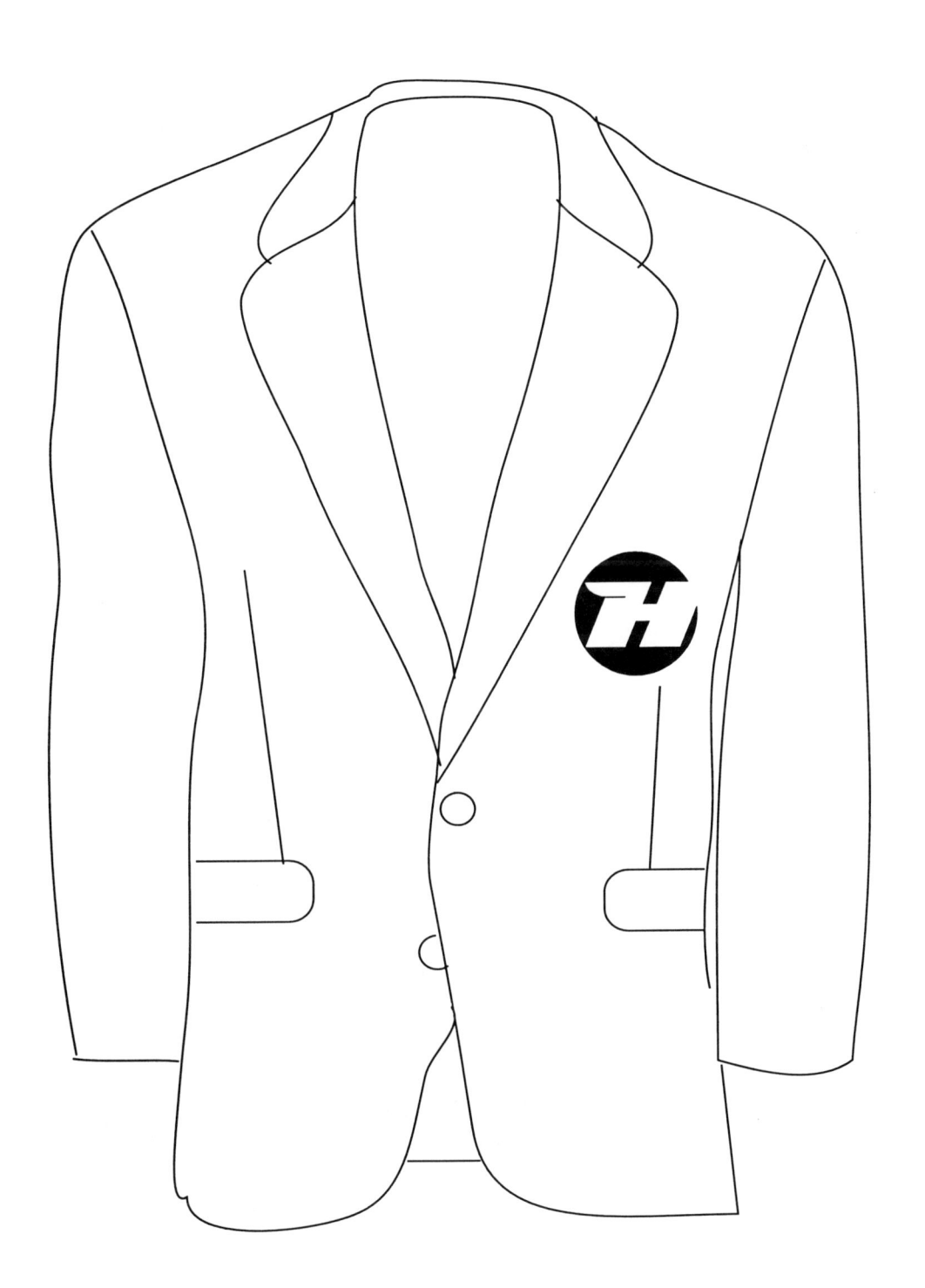

Only vehicles that are used exclusively inside company property are to use the logo alone. All others are exposed to thousands of people every day, and are to include both the name and logo.

77

Company signage will be seen by thousands of people daily. Therefore, it is important to use the logo and name together. Due to the shape of the sign, it is impossible to use the "logo at left" arrangement that is preferred, so the stacked version is used.

Chapter 12
Legal Aspects of Logo Design

This is not going to be a long chapter, nor is it intended to take the place of legal services by an attorney specializing in trademark law. The purpose of this chapter is to give you a short fundamental introduction to the legal aspects of logo design, and to make you aware of some of the pitfalls that await the unwary designer.

First of all, you should know that from a legal point of view, a trademark's mission is to "identify and distinguish," the goods or services of one entity from that of another producer of goods or services, and to indicate the source of the goods or services.

Second, regarding logos and company names, just because you can register a name or logo at the state (or even federal) level, that does not mean that you have absolute right to it. The law does not allow clerks in the Secretary of States' offices to make final legal decision on who has rights to what trademark or name. The courts are the final arbiter of such matters.

With our current legal system regarding names and logos, common law ownership of a name or logo can override legal claims to even a registered trade mark, whether it be a name or logo.

If you aren't confused by now, just wait.

Basically, legal disputes concerning trademark rights are decided in a court of law, where "priority of use" and "likelihood of confusion" are the principal inquiries. In such areas, "legal precedent" often is of little value. Each case is decided on its own merits, and that can lead to some surprising results for the uninformed or ill advised. The real meaning of this is that there are no "sure things" in trademark disputes.

Friendly warning. Some practical advice. OK. You have a computer, a lot of graphics software and a client down the street who wants to open a little restaurant. You start playing on the screen, and suddenly come up with a couple of arches. "They would look nice in a yellowish gold," you say to yourself. Don't even think about it. Kill the thought, right here and now. **The major message to remember is:** just because you create something on your computer, that doesn't mean that your client has a right to use it.

In one of the most notorious trademark cases in history, NBC announced a new logo in 1976 (a stylized "N"), and immediately discovered that it was virtually identical to the design that was being used by the Nebraska Educational TV network. Even though NBC had done a massive search of registered trademarks, the Nebraska logo did not appear, since it had not been registered. However, the Nebraska people had prior "common law" rights to the logo, and NBC was faced with the embarrassing (and expensive) situation of having to purchase the rights to its new logo from a small operation in the Midwest. Before you become paranoid about legal problems and decide to abandon the thought of doing logos at all, let's look at the other side of the coin. If you exercise just a little caution and forethought, you can be fairly sure you won't have any insurmountable legal problems with logos you create. The primary consideration in trademark liability is "likelihood of confusion." This principle involves inquiry into a number of factors (your lawyer can tell you which), and is to be determined through the eyes of the hypothetical ordinary prudent purchaser for products of that kind. With the "likelihood of confusion" test in mind, here are a few guidelines to follow.

1. If you somehow design a logo for a radio station in Nantucket, Massachusetts, and later discover that it's similar to a design for a beauty shop in Las Vegas, Nevada, it may not really be a legal problem. (Due to the different target consumers and geographic differences, there is no overlap in the market areas, therefore, no likelihood of confusion.

2. On the other hand, if you design a logo for a local savings & loan, and somehow get a design that looks like one for a regional banking group with offices in a neighboring state, you better do something else. (The bank's logo has pre-existing rights, and the bank's anticipated or reasonable area of future expansion could include your area. Your logo would likely infringe on theirs.)

3. If you're designing a logo for a regional or national firm, one way to avoid possible infringement (with an unknown entity, as in the NBC case) is to create a composite design combining both the logo and business name in type, or simply stylizing the type. (See the Navix logo on page 120 for an example.)

Information for this chapter was supplied by James R. Higgins, Jr., an attorney who practices considerable trade mark law. Contact: James R. Higgins, Jr., Middleton & Reutlinger, 2500 Brown & Williamson Tower, Louisville, KY 40202 (502) 584-1135.

Part 2 - Logo Examples

Chapter 13
Using the Computer Tools to Create Logos

      This chapter includes a fairly comprehensive overview of the drawing tools that are included in most drawing programs. Even if you're already an experienced computer artist, skim this section anyway. You may get a new idea or two. And if you've just enlisted in the computer graphics revolution, this section will give you a good feel for some of the type things you can do.

      The following chapter shows a large number of examples of logos done using the tools available in drawing programs. I suggest you try some of these techniques. The more you experiment (and practice) the faster you'll be able to do great logos.

Blending Colors/ Graduated Fill

The blend tool allows you to blend shades or grey as shown here, and is an especially a nice way to blend colors (*not* shown here, since this is a black and white book.)

You can normally apply a blend to any solid object, even those with irregular shapes. The blend at top (long rectangle) is done on an even plane. At right is an example of a graduated fill at an angle, and the example at the bottom shows a graduated fill that has a lighter center and darker edges. There are many options for using these two techniques. Check your drawing program's instruction manual for more details on this feature.

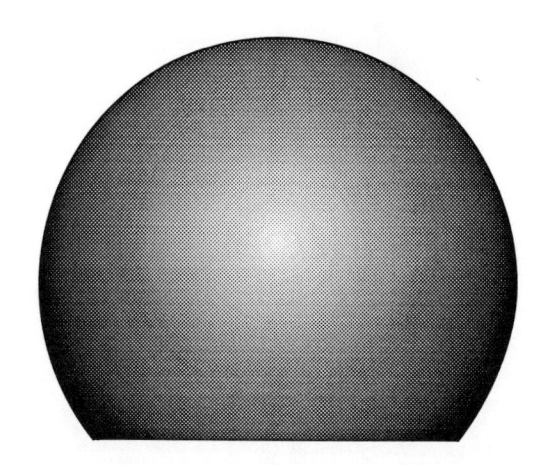

Blending Stripes & Lines

Blending stripes and lines is a really nice feature of most drawing programs that lets you do some really creative graphics instantly.

To create the series of lines at the bottom, I started with these two lines here. They're copies of each other, and are placed on the same horizontal plane.

To create this, I simply used the "blend" feature of FreeHand, specified that I wanted 10 intermediate steps, the 10 new lines were automatically put into place.

These two elements are mirror images of each other.

To create this nice look, I once again used the "blend" feature, specified 7 intermediate steps, and the middle elements were put into position immediately.

85

Blending Shapes

Shapes can also be blended. I began with the tall oval at the left, and the near circle at the right.

By using the "blend" feature of FreeHand, I was able to let the computer insert the middle three elements. Note that the new elements are a progression of change from the original tall oval to the final design at right.

This design is really a good example of what you can create with blended shapes. I started with the top and bottom shapes. "Blending" created all the shapes in between. "Blend" made the flying sea gull design come to life very accurately, creating an animation look.

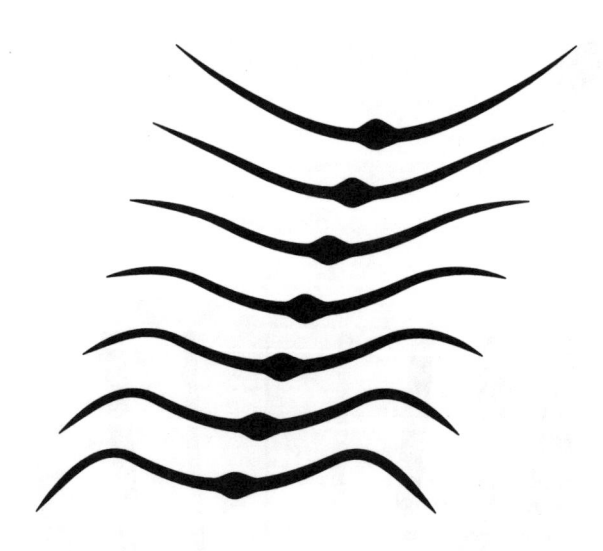

Rotate

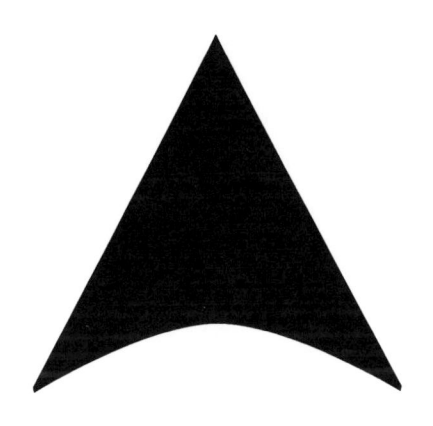

All the drawing programs allow you to "rotate" an object. You simply have to specify the number of degrees the element is to be moved.

The design at left was made by rotating the simple triangle at top and then adding a series of parallel lines.

87

Rotate/Duplicate

You can begin with the rotation tool (last page), and then use the drawing program's ability to duplicate a move multiple times. The nice design below was created in less than a minute. It all started with the design element shown at right.

The next step was to clone the element. Then, I chose "rotate" and specified 20 degrees, and moved the cloned element. Then I duplicated the move until I had the full design with 18 individual elements.

Type Changed to Art

Type

Type

Many of the drawing programs have a feature which allows you to change type into art. That is, the letters are changed into graphic images, so you can make any changes you wish. For example I started with the word "Type" at top. I converted it to art, then altered the "T" and "p" to create the design at left.

Note: Not all type can be converted to art, and not all drawing programs have this feature. However, there is a program for the Macintosh called Altsys Metamorphosis Professional that will convert virtually any type into art that may be edited.

Here's another example of changing type to art. This started off as a normal word set in type. I converted it, then changed each of its letters in some way to come up with a totally unusual treatment of the name.

Twixt

Duplicate Move

The "duplicate move" feature of most drawing programs allows you to do precision placement of identical images to create graphics. This design's major element is the wave shown at the top of the page.

To get the look at right, I simply drew a black circle, then changed the "wave" to white. Next, I put the wave on top of the circle, cloned the wave, and moved the clone down into its desired position. By duplicating the move several times, I was able to add all the extra waves with total precision in less than a minute.

Duplicate Move & Change Size

You can also duplicate a move and change the size of the element at the same time. I began with the simple element at the top of the page.

Next I cloned it, reduced its height (now its width) by 20%, then moved the element. By duplicating the move several times, I created this design in less than a minute.

Rotate, Duplicate & Change Size

You can also duplicate and change size while you rotate an object. The design at bottom started off with a single vertical rectangle (the big one shown at right). Next, I cloned it, and rotated the clone. The result of the first few "duplicate move" commands is shown at top.

I kept duplicating the move many times, then when I had the look I wanted, I grouped the entire piece and rotated it into is final position shown at bottom.

Mirror Image

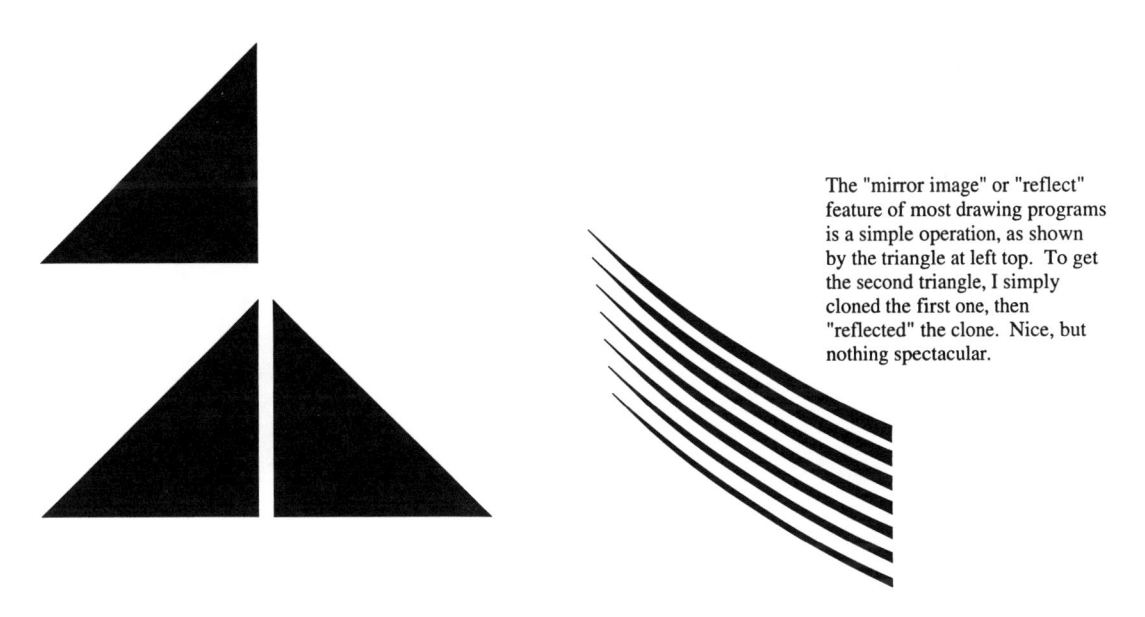

The "mirror image" or "reflect" feature of most drawing programs is a simple operation, as shown by the triangle at left top. To get the second triangle, I simply cloned the first one, then "reflected" the clone. Nice, but nothing spectacular.

This "reflect" feature becomes a handy tool when you create a graphic like the one just above, and you want an exact mirror image to match with it. That's what I did, and the result is shown at the bottom of the page.

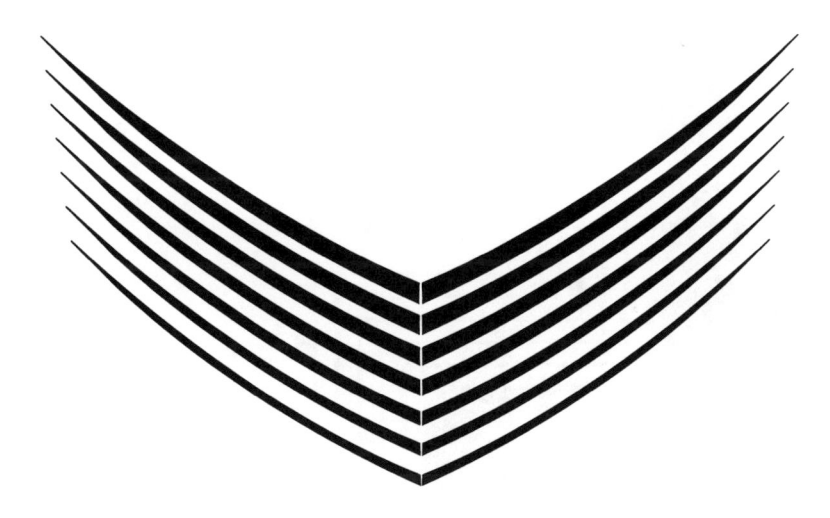

93

Clone & Move; Duplicate

This ability will really help you make precision graphics that would be very difficult to accomplish on a drawing board. The design at right started with the simple angled element at left. It was then cloned and moved, and then the move was duplicated several times.

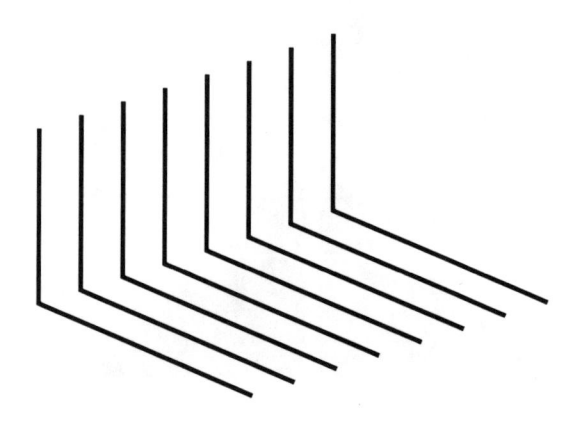

The design at right used the same technique as the one above, except the letter "L" was used as a foundation. The first angled line was done to match the shape of the "L,"

Clone & Move; Change Line

Simple cloning and moving takes on a new dimension when you change the color of some of the objects afterwards. At top, the individual elements were changed to progressively lighter shades of grey, while the design at the bottom has alternating elements changed to grey.

Patterned Type

Most of the drawing programs have the ability to insert a large number of patterns inside type, or other drawn objects.

Regular

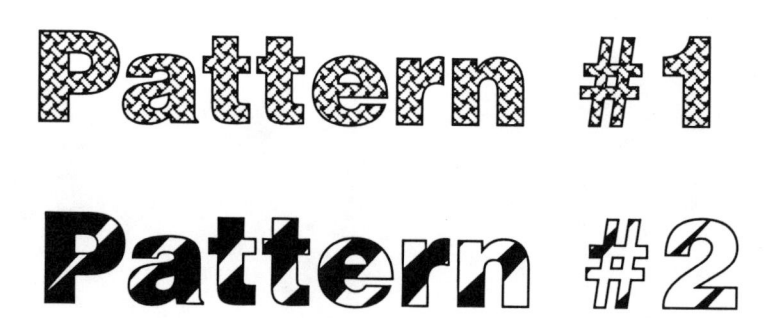

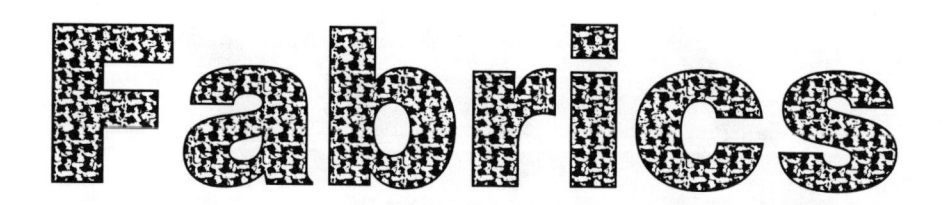

Pattern #1

Pattern #2

Fabrics

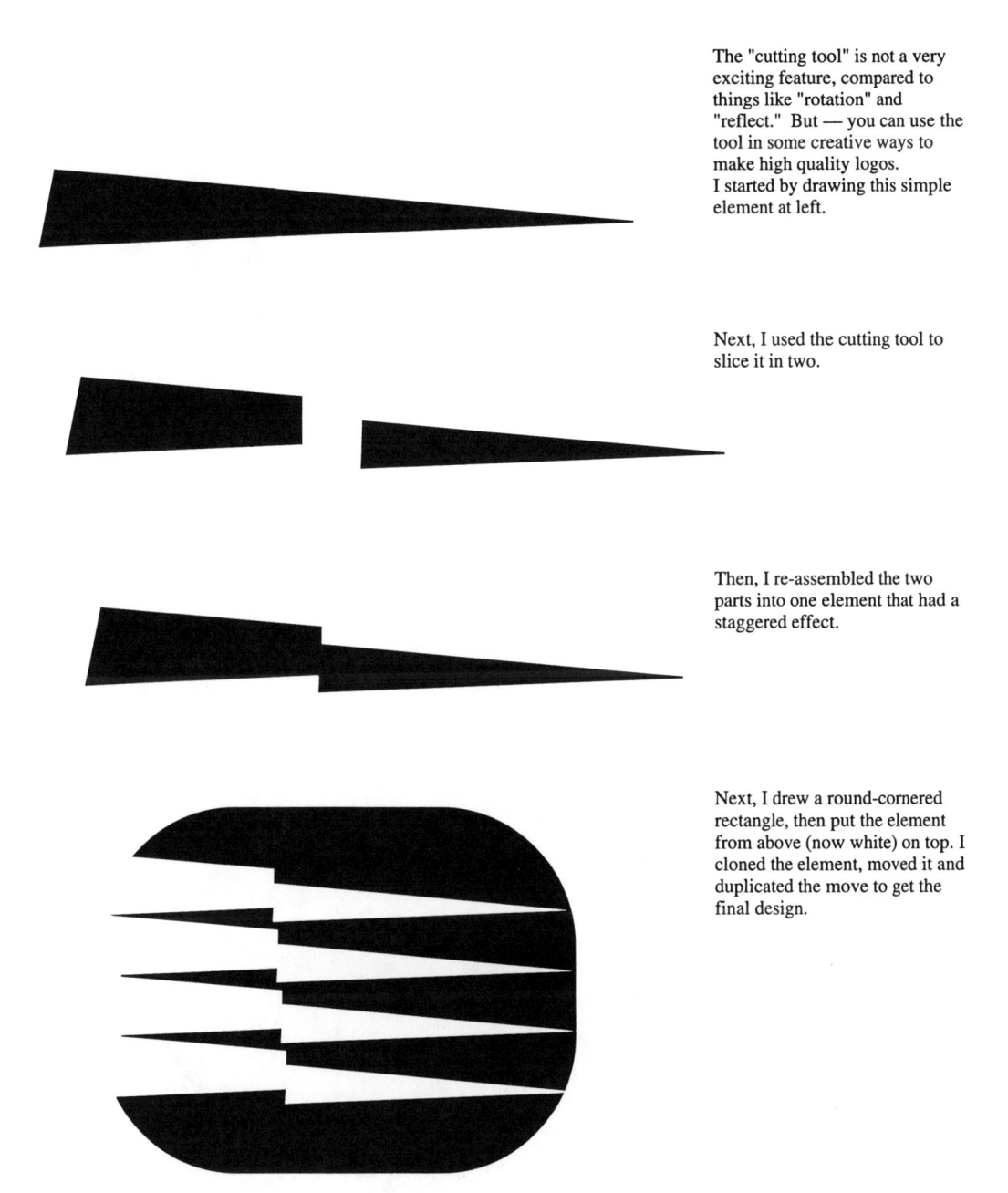

The Cutting Tool

The "cutting tool" is not a very exciting feature, compared to things like "rotation" and "reflect." But — you can use the tool in some creative ways to make high quality logos.
I started by drawing this simple element at left.

Next, I used the cutting tool to slice it in two.

Then, I re-assembled the two parts into one element that had a staggered effect.

Next, I drew a round-cornered rectangle, then put the element from above (now white) on top. I cloned the element, moved it and duplicated the move to get the final design.

Variable Line Thickness

One of the most useful features of drawing programs allows you to change the thickness of lines. The lines shown here range in thickness from 1/2 point to 36 points. You can apply "line thickness" directions to straight lines, curved lines, irregular lines, etc.

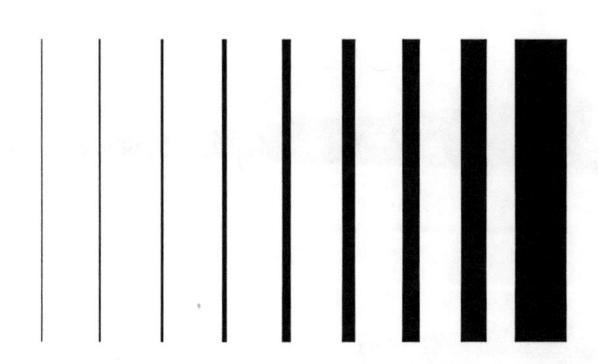

Here, I created this interesting graphic simply by having several overlapping circular arcs of different lengths. Each one has a different line thickness.

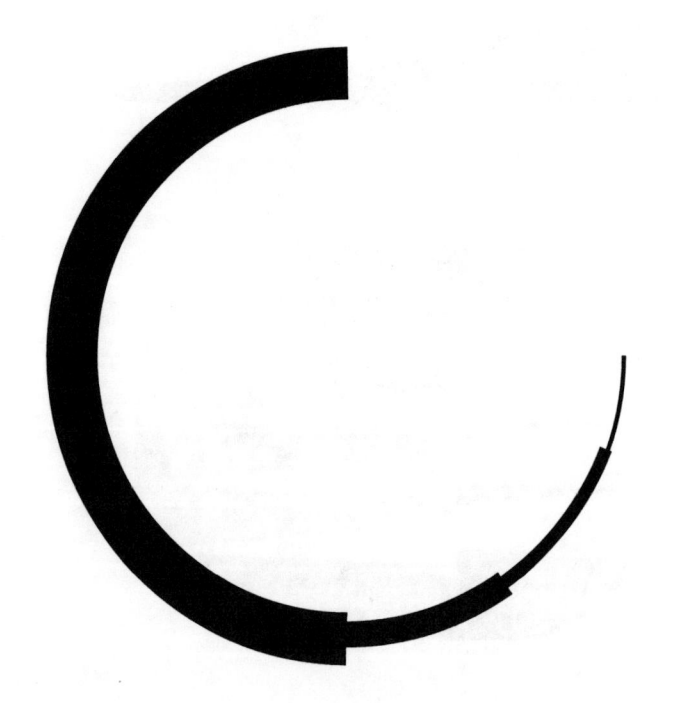

Shadow Effect

Shadow effects are created very easily. Begin with a black rectangle. Then copy the rectangle, change the "fill" of the copy to white, then position the white one on top of the black at the desired angle.

To get this look, do the same thing as above, only use an oval.

Skewing

Skewing an object gives it an "italic" slant. You can skew elements to any angle you wish. At right, you see a before and after example of a normal rectangle. That's not particularly impressive, but only because the design is so simple.

Normal

Skewed

The real ability of the skewing tool is shown by seeing this design element in its original form at right ... and when it is skewed and placed onto a circular background at the bottom.

When used with abstract elements, skewing can dramatically change the appearance of a graphic.

Uneven Scaling

The "scaling" tool lets you enlarge or reduce an element by a certain percentage. However, it also lets you change the horizontal or vertical size independently of the other dimension. To illustrate this, I started off with the square at top. Then, I *enlarged its width* to 300% of original size, while *reducing its height* to 50% of the original. The result is the changed square is shown at right.

A good example of using this irregular scaling is shown with this logo. The design element at left is the bottom element in the logo. You can see how the other similar elements in the logo were reduced in height while maintaining their common width.

101

Type on Curved Path

Type on a curved path

FreeHand and some other drawing programs have a feature that allows you to join type to an irregularly shaped line.

The line of type at the top was set first. Then, the line at right was drawn. I selected both of the elements, then chose "join elements," and the type immediately took on the shape of the line.

You can draw line of virtually any shape and use this feature.

Type on a curved path

The Bell-Shaped Curve, Inc

PostScript Effects

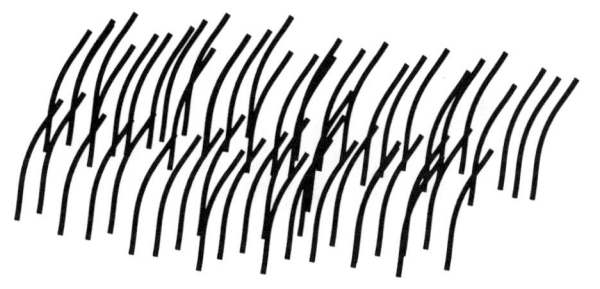

200 randomgrass

200 = number of blades

FreeHand (and some other programs have a feature called "PostScript effects" which take a little extra time to create, but can be worth it.

To do these items, you have to actually type in a code phrase, such as *200 randomgrass* or *10 45 0 1 tigerteeth*. Seems a bit complicated, but it's well explained in the FreeHand manual. Examples of random grass and tigerteeth are shown on this page.

10 45 0 1 tigerteeth

10 = number of teeth
45 = rotation angle
0 = teeth color
1 = background color

Shadow Type Face

Shadow

There's nothing complicated about shadow effects for type. All the drawing programs have the feature as part of "type specs," and most page layout programs such as PageMaker also have this same ability. However, just because something is simple doesn't mean that it can't be used effectively. Don't forget about these type specs. Use them when appropriate.

Midnight

Outline Type

OUTLINE

Everything I just said on the opposite page also applies here.

Chattanooga

Condensed Type

When you want a type that is more condensed than is available in the normal font options, you can create highly condensed (see "The Sardine Can") image by simply "grouping" the type, then squeezing it into a tighter vertical space.

Condensed

The Sardine Can

Extended Type

When you want a more extended type than is available in the normal font options, simply "group" the type and stretch it to the desired width.

Extended

Long Line

Before & After

Now that you have seen most of the tools offered by your drawing program, let me offer an unsolicited endorsement for a great publication that will give you great tips on how to get the most out of those tools.

Before & After is a 16-page, full color periodical that is well worth the money. Use only one of its techniques, and you've paid for a year's worth of issues. They didn't ask for this space. But I think anyone who uses any drawing program should subscribe to Before & After. It includes things that no other publication has.

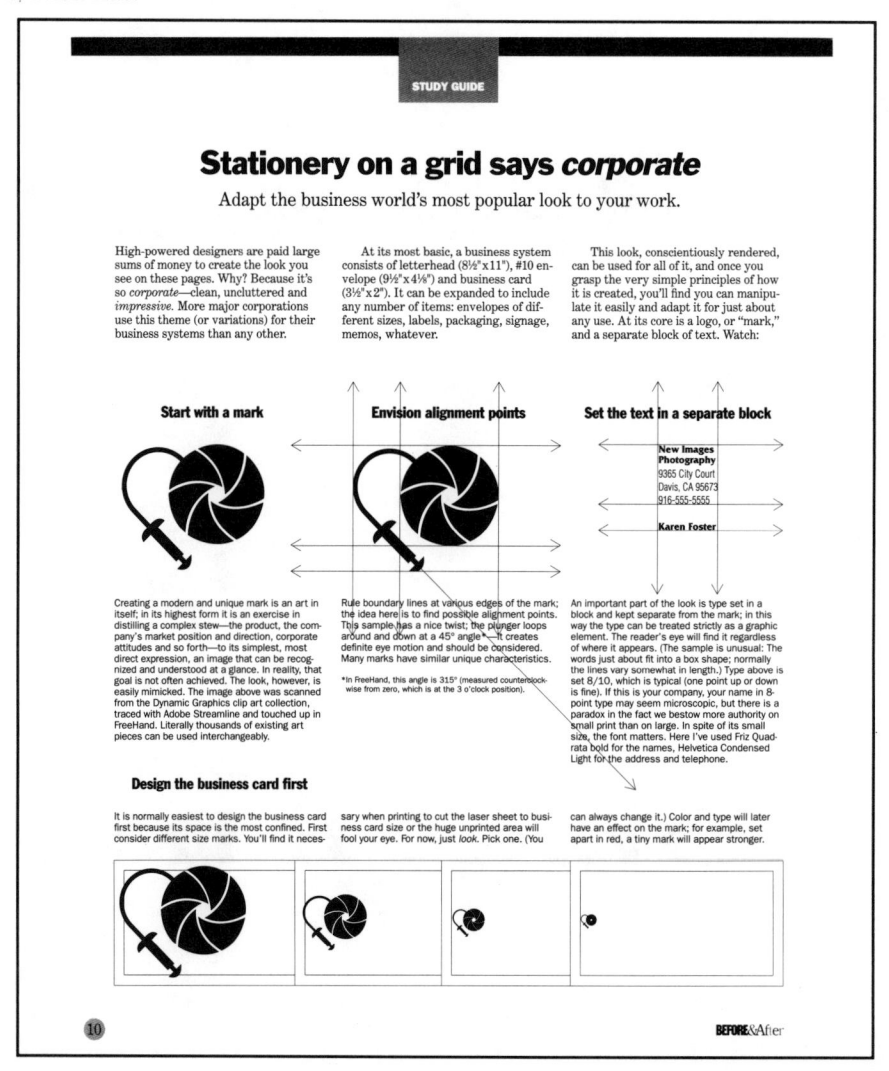

Now, move around on a grid

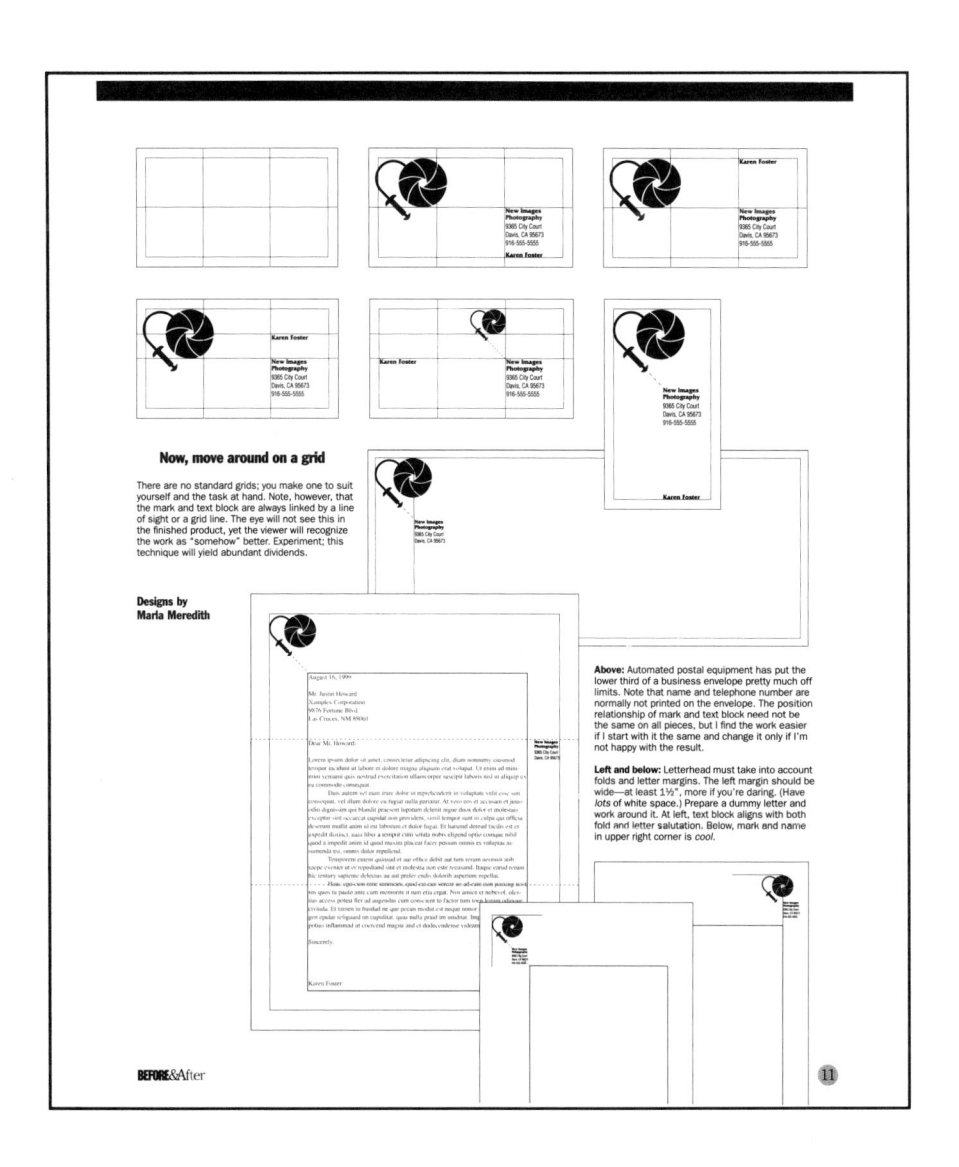

There are no standard grids; you make one to suit yourself and the task at hand. Note, however, that the mark and text block are always linked by a line of sight or a grid line. The eye will not see this in the finished product, yet the viewer will recognize the work as "somehow" better. Experiment; this technique will yield abundant dividends.

Designs by
Marla Meredith

Above: Automated postal equipment has put the lower third of a business envelope pretty much off limits. Note that name and telephone number are normally not printed on the envelope. The position relationship of mark and text block need not be the same on all pieces, but I find the work easier if I start with it the same and change it only if I'm not happy with the result.

Left and below: Letterhead must take into account folds and letter margins. The left margin should be wide—at least 1½", more if you're daring. (Have *lots* of white space.) Prepare a dummy letter and work around it. At left, text block aligns with both fold and letter salutation. Below, mark and name in upper right corner is *cool*.

Before & After is a publication of PageLab, Inc. 331 J Street, Suite 150, Sacramento, CA 95814-9671. Phone (916) 443-4890.

109

Chapter 14
Some Logo Design Formats
(a great idea starter)

This section includes a large number of logos, all of which were done on a computer using a drawing program. This section is actually done for two diverse audiences:

• the beginning computer artist. For this reader, a detailed description of how the design was created is included. This will give the novice a good feel for the computer logo creation process.

• the experienced computer artist. The logos in this section are a great idea starter, and should serve as inspiration for the designer who has been working on a computer for a while.

Name Inside Shape

This is among the simplest type of logo designs. To get this effect, I used TypeStyler to make the name, and then simply made an oval from the FreeHand toolbox to fit around the name.

I made the original triangle (the outer one, then cloned and reduced it to make the two smaller ones. Then, I simply set the type inside and centered it.

Name as a Shape

BASS-BOAT

The fish shape is a standard menu item in TypeStyler, a terrific program that is discussed in more detail on page 218.

WINNERS

Another job done with the help of TypeStyler. This "pennant" style is one of the many options in the program, and can be done in just a minute or so.

Logo and Name Inside Shape

Begin with a round-cornered rectangle. Put the bear inside. Put the type inside. Instant logo.

Another instant logo.

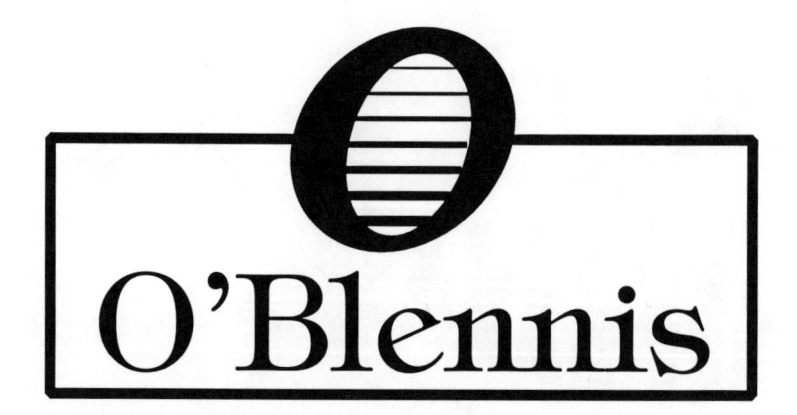

Graphic Under Name

Mid-American

The name on top of a graphic offers many visual options. Use your imagination and see what you can come up with in this format.

Thunder!

White Name on Dark Base Object

There are many shapes which can serve as a base object. This pentagon was a good choice for the name Penta. I thought the design was enhanced by having the first and last letters bleed off the edge of the design.

The water drop with waves at the bottom nicely frames the name Aqua.

Name and Abstract Graphic on Base

Both these use abstract designs along with the name on a bold base object.

Modified Type - One Letter as Logo

This is the logo for a large health care company in Bangkok, Thailand. The logo design at right is a modified letter V, which gives the name a distinctive name when used in this way.

The other design below is an optional use which takes the first letter of the top symbol and makes it a logo unto itself. Note that the name is always used with the "V" logo below.

Vitacor

V

Vitacor

Name in Contrasting Type Faces

The contrast of the two types is heightened by the insertion of the capitol dome in between the words.

LAW & ORDER

The stark contrast of the two fonts make this a bold, striking identifier for a periodical publication.

Corporate **ID**

Name with Secondary Graphic

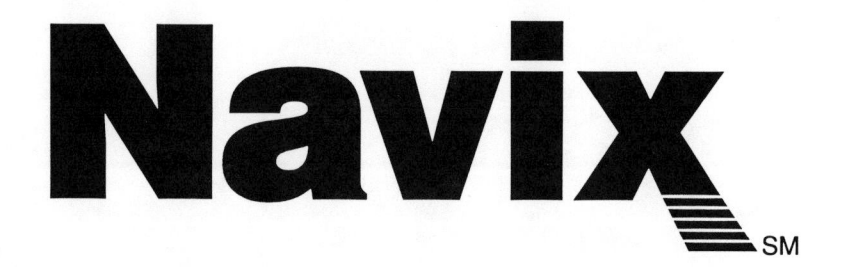

Navix ℠

This design was done for national use. In similar cases, a "wordmark" is often used to minimize potential trademark infringement cases.

Silicon

The use of visual alterations to a name is a nice alternative to simply using the name set in a common type face.

Three Dimensional Symbol

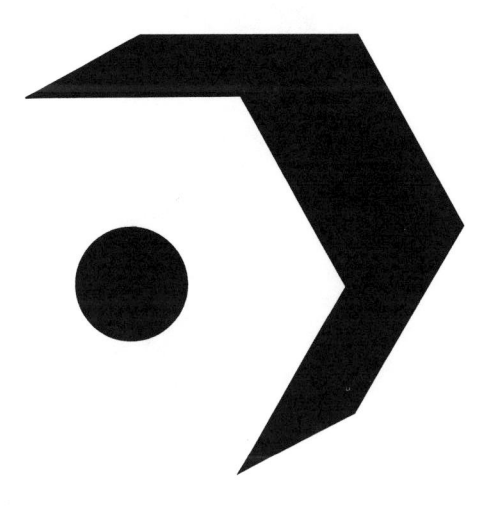

To get this shadow effect, I first created the 6-sided design (which is now white). Then, I drew the lines that would extend back to create the dimensional area. Finally, I added the black circle to create the feeling an a hole.

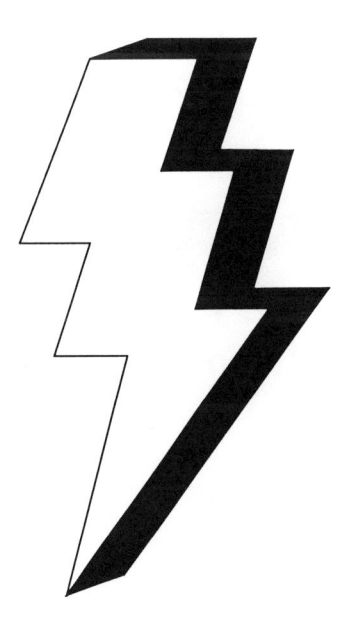

This logo started off as a bolt of lightning — a black bolt of lightning. I then cloned it, turned the clone white, and added the thin line on the left edge. At first tried it with no line at left, but it didn't look right. The thin line really helped it.

121

Three Dimensional Letter

This design wasn't all that difficult to do. The bold front of the "O" was made from the edge line of a tall oval.. I simply cut the edge, cloned it, moved the clone to the left, and drew straight lines to connect the two edges. I applied the black oval center and added an appropriate type face to finish the design.

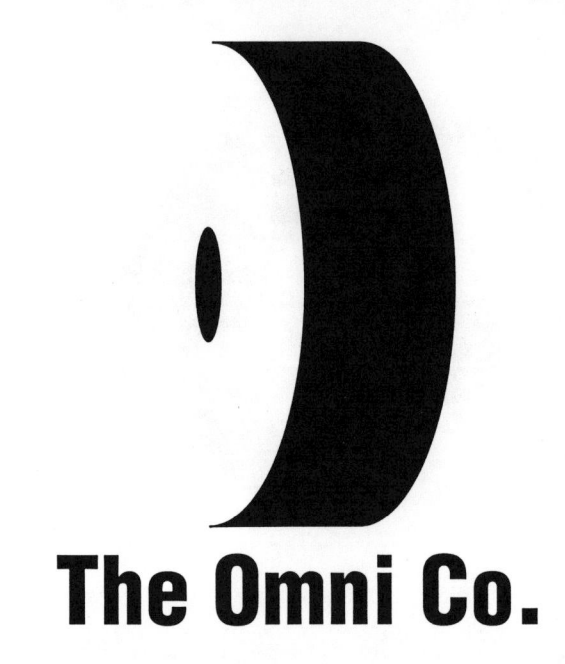

The Omni Co.

This started with the letter N. I changed it to art, then revised its shape to suit my idea of what the finished design should be. Next, I drew angled lines to create the shadow background. Once that was completed, I changed the original N to white, and had a nice looking design.

Name as Background

This is a style that I really like that has a lot of possible graphic options. To get this look, I set the name, then created one "blade of grass." I then copied the grass numerous times and put each one into the desired position to finish.

The word "zoo" isn't actually type. The two "O" letters are black circles, and I drew the ""Z" to match the height and weight of the circles. I used pre-drawn animals, turned them white and quickly had a very nice design.

123

Name Positive/Negative Letters

This design started with the name set in Helvetica Black. After ungrouping the letters, I changed the "O" and "A" to white, and then changed the negative space on those letters to black. Once that was done, it was a simple matter to move the letters to produce the overlap that makes this visual interesting.

Gimme a "D." Gimme an "E." Gimme an "&." Make the & white. What do you have? A good cheer and a nice design.

Symbol Positive/Negative

The Food Chain

I started with the big fish. Made a copy of it, 50% of original size, and turned it white. Then, I made a copy of the second fish, which was again reduced 50%. The smallest fish was changed to black, I set type and had a nice visual.

Once the original cross was made, I cloned and moved it until I had 5 different crosses in a line. But they were all black, so I changed the second and fourth ones to white, which finished the logo.

Kaleidoscope

This is an example of a design done using the clone and rotate feature. Once all the "spokes" were complete, I added the initial to the middle.

This rather complex-looking design is actually made up of a whole bunch of elements like the one shown above. I used the same technique as the upper logo: clone and repeat. Then, I put a black circle in the center to use as a base for the white type.

Flag Look

This design started off as a black circle. I then added one "flag wave" element, cloned and moved it, and duplicated the process until the circle was covered with flag stripes.

American Pie

The flag waves are totally different from those in the above design, and give a totally different feeling. Each of the three stripes is identical. Once the three were in place, I added the type, being careful to place the word "Pie" so that it would have some white space below.

Stars as Base Object

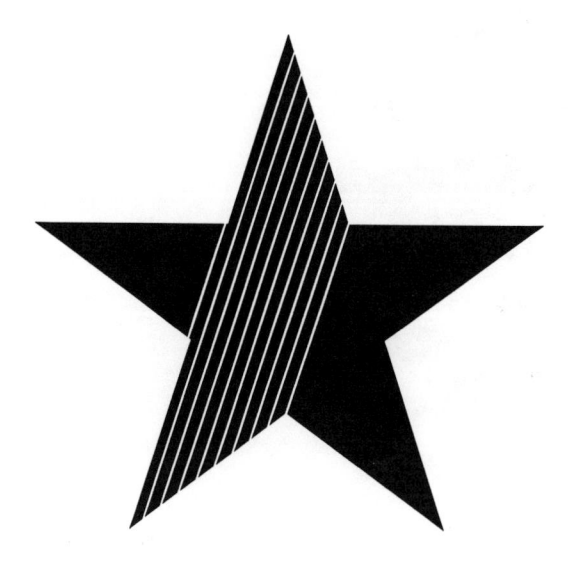

This simple star is made into a nice design just by adding a series of parallel stipes to fill a natural segment of the design.

This star began just like the one above. Then, I ungrouped it, and moved the points so that it was much thinner. Then, I added the white vertical lines to finish.

Product as Main Visual

photos by Lauren

This logo for a photographer uses a simple but bold base graphic: the end of a film roll. The design is completed by adding reversed type.

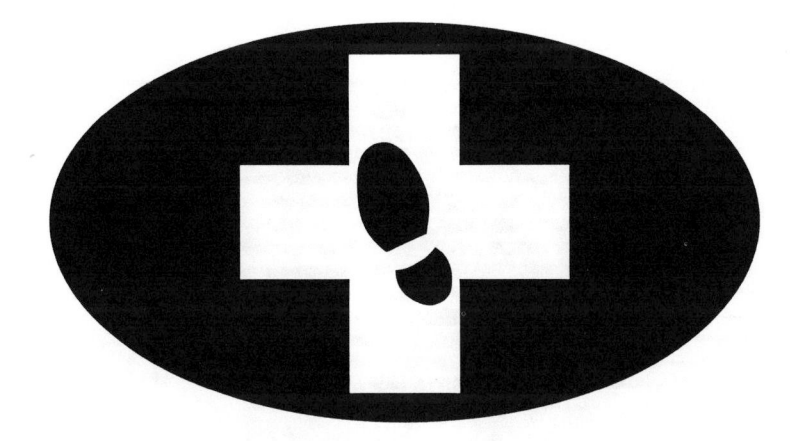

The Shoe Doctor

This shoe repair shop needed a design which would primarily be used as a sign to attract attention from a distance. We began with a red oval, then put the white medical cross on top, and finished the design with a shoe track in the center. The type at the bottom leaves no doubt about the name of the business.

Space Age Graphics

The computer tools allow for the quick, precise rendering of graphic effects such as those shown at right. This design was created by starting with the design element at the top; then it was cloned and repeated down the page, with a reduction in horizontal size being done with each step.

This design was originally done to fit within a perfect circle. However, when it was completed, it was "skewed" to get the desired speed effect.

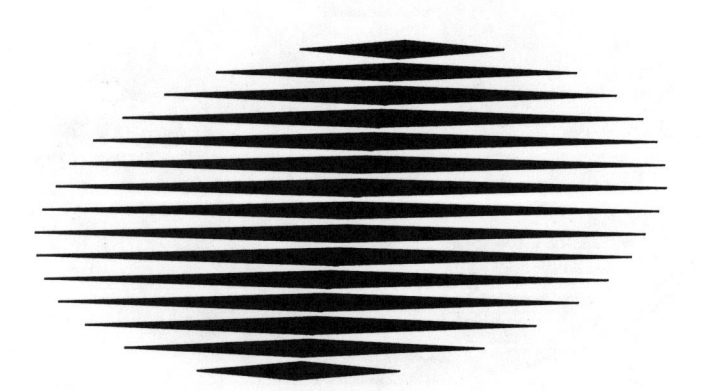

The Family Look

No. Not **that** kind of family.

Siegel Group

When a designer wants to show that several businesses have a common ownership, a graphic system is created which will have a common element. In this sample, the logo for the Siegel Group is used for each business, along with the same type face for each of the variations.

Siegel Group Real Estate, Inc.

Siegel Group Insurance, Inc.

Miller

Foil

Fossils

Another way to show common ownership is shown here. The Miller name features the lower-case letter L done as a logo inside the name. The same design is featured in the words Foliage and Fossils.

Venetian Blinds

The look that I call "venetian blinds" is easily done. This logo starts with a circle, drawn from the toolbox. Then, the black lines are added. The final step is to clone the black lines, change them to white, and then move them down into position.

This nice design was done with a variation of the venetian blind look. The left side of the N simply has white lines positioned over the base of the letter. For the right side, the white lines are smaller than the black ones.

132

Rough Sketch Look

For people who think computer design looks "too mechanical," here is a logo which is highly informal, but was drawn on the Macintosh with FreeHand.

Here's another informal design which was done by computer. To get the precise line thickness on the drawing board would take a while. This pencil was done in about a minute and a half.

Dots as Graphic

To analyze how this design was done, let's look at only one line of dots at a time. The top line was done by simply creating the left dot and the right dot, then using the "blend" feature of FreeHand to create the dots in between. Next, each dot was given a specific value of grey — anywhere from 10% to 80%. Then, to complete the design, the line of dots was cloned and moved below the original top line. This was repeated several times to complete the design as shown.

Again, to see how this logo was done, we need to break the process down into small steps. Once the square was done, the center line (vertical) of dots was done first. The top dot was drawn from the toolbox, then the large center dot was done. The dots in between were created with the "blend" feature of FreeHand. This made a line of six dots, with the largest one at the bottom. Then, the six dots were grouped and cloned. The cloned image was then rotated so that it made the symmetrical vertical line of dots that you now see in the center. The same steps were followed to create the other vertical lines of dots. Try this; it's easier than it looks.

Steen Paints

134

Parallel Lines

This is a nice look that is very easy to create. First, you draw a rectangle something like the one at the left. Next, you skew it to give it the angle. Then, clone the shape, move it to the right and change it into a more narrow shape. Then, use the "blend" feature to make the shapes in between.

After the circle was drawn, the white line at the extreme left was done in a 3 point width. Then, the thicker white line at far right was done in 12 points. Next, the blend feature was used to create all the lines in between.

Silhouette

Once a basic image is done, it is very easy to create this look. We started with the dolphin in black, then made a clone of the original, which was then changed to white. Another copy of the black original was made, and then the 3 images were spaced properly to achieve the final design.

Here's a different way to create silhouettes. This "family" is actually composed of a man and a woman. The "kids" are simply reduced versions of their parents; the kids' "fill" was simply changed to white.

Pixel Look

This logo started with a star as the base object. Next, 900 squares (a 30 x 30 matrix grid of small squares) were placed on top of the star. The squares that were not wanted were deleted, and those on top of the star were changed to white.

A "D" in Helvetica Bold was the base object for this design. Then, the first line of small squares was done, using the "blend" feature of FreeHand. The completed top line was cloned and moved, and the steps were duplicated to achieve the line of graphics extending back from the D. Finally, the boxes which overlapped the base letter were changed to white.

Curved Type

The diamond background is simply a square drawn from the toolbox and then rotated 45 degrees. The baseball was drawn by using circles. Finally, the type was done in TypeStyler and placed on top.

This is just one of the variety of type configurations that is done very simply in the TypeStyler program.

Grid as Background

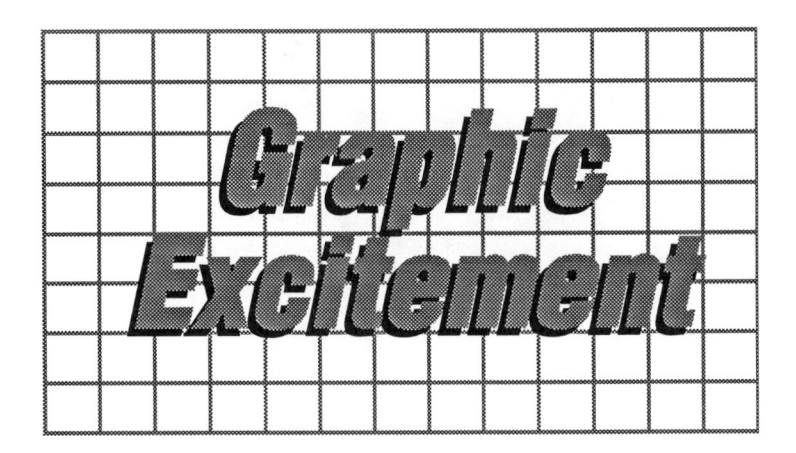

The foundation for this design is the background grid, which was created simply and accurately with the "copy and repeat" feature available in most drawing programs. Next, the type was done, and it was then copied, moved slightly and changed in color to give it the shadow effect,

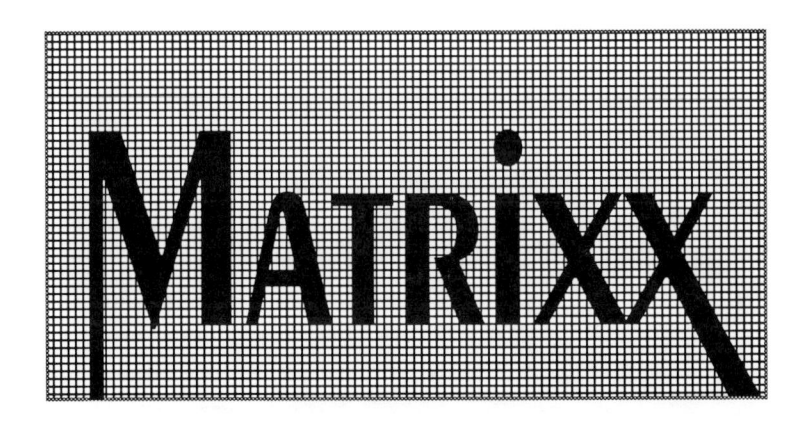

The grid here was done with a tighter background to give it a very different look from the design above. After the type was placed on top, we used the "convert to paths" feature of FreeHand which allowed us to achieve the flowing look of the first and last letters.

Variable Thickness Lines

The base of this design is a round cornered rectangle done from the toolbox. The top effect was done first, then the bottom effect was put into place. Finally, the "blend" feature was used to create the middle four elements.

This interesting design was really very simple to produce. Once the top element was drawn, it was cloned and moved three times. This created the top half of the design, which was simply copied and flipped into position.

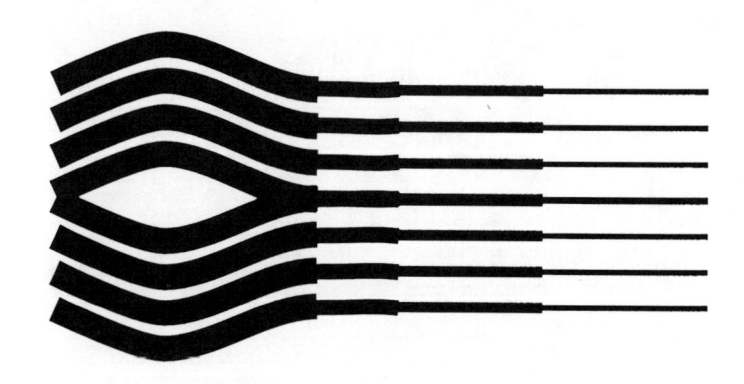

Complex Symmetry

With the computer's abilities, creating complex symmetry designs is really very simple. This logo started with the star as a base object. Next, the first white line at left was drawn. Note that it's simply an angled line. That line was then cloned and moved, and the action was repeated a number of times to complete half of the effect. That half was then copied and flipped to finish the right half of the design.

Once the oval was drawn, the white effect at the left was drawn. (Note that it's simply a very tall triangle.) The effect was then copied and moved along an arc that aligned with the top of the oval. Multiple repeats of this step completed the left half of the design. Then, the effect was copied and flipped to complete the logo.

Base with Variable Thickness Lines

To start this design, I began by scanning an outline of Texas to be used as a guideline. Next, I placed the thick/thin lines across the state, starting at the top and working my way down. Each line is thin outside the state's border, and becomes thicker inside the boundary. Once I had the idea for this, the entire project took me about 45 minutes. Doing this the old way on a drawing board might have taken a good artist about 20 to 30 hours (It would have taken *me* about a year, allowing time for correcting spilled ink and smudges.)

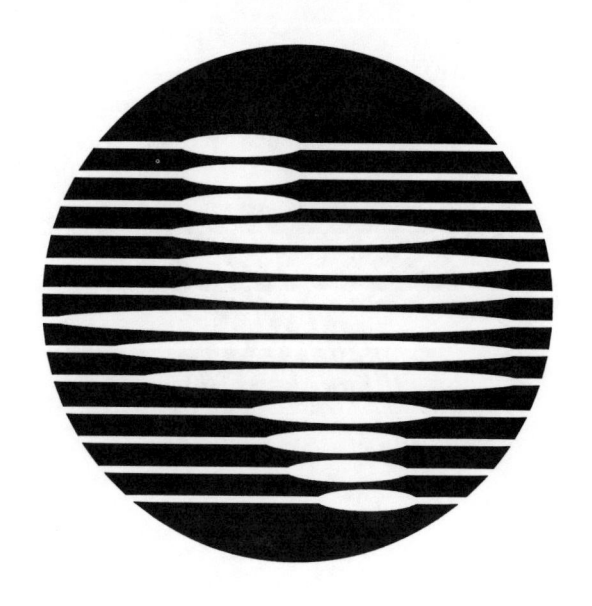

This was done in a similar way to the "Texas" logo above. However, note that each white element in the design actually tapers off to the right. This technique lets you create some very interesting logos with a minimum of time spent.

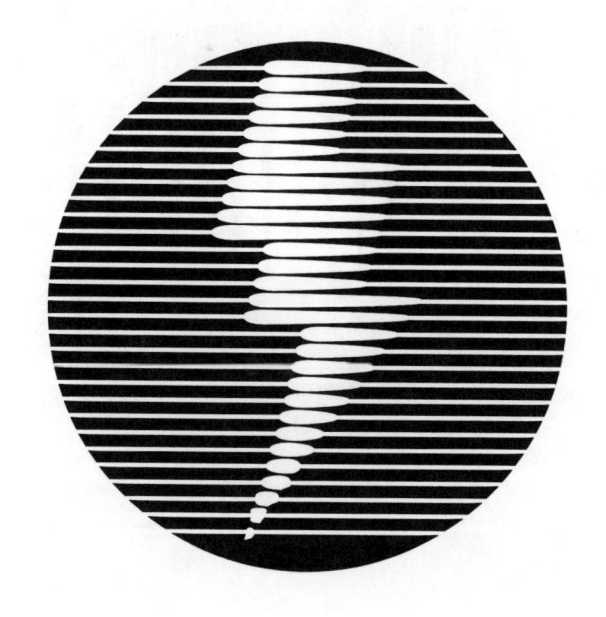

142

Directional Sign Look

The outline shape was drawn as a rounded square, then rotated 45 degrees. Next, the airplane shape was drawn, and the type was added.

This is a nice design done with a minimum amount of effort. Both the octagon-shaped base object and the cat outline came from Logo SuperPower. Then, the type was placed on top to complete the design in about three minutes.

Southwestern Look

Take a look at the "Aztec Motel" type. This actually started off as Helvetica Bold. I simply ungrouped the type and deleted the points which weren't needed for the look I wanted.

The two graphic elements were done quickly on FreeHand. The beauty of the Southwestern look is that you don't have to be especially precise in your design elements.

The center of the sun started as a perfect circle. It was ungrouped and the points moved slightly to give it the irregular shape.

The sunbursts were all made from one basic design: an oval that was ungrouped and changed in the same way as the sun. I then used the rotate/repeat feature of FreeHand (15 degree increments) to make them rotate around the sun. Then, I moved each one and changed its shape slightly to achieve the hand-drawn look. Finally, the type was placed in the center with no modifications.

Hand Lettered Look

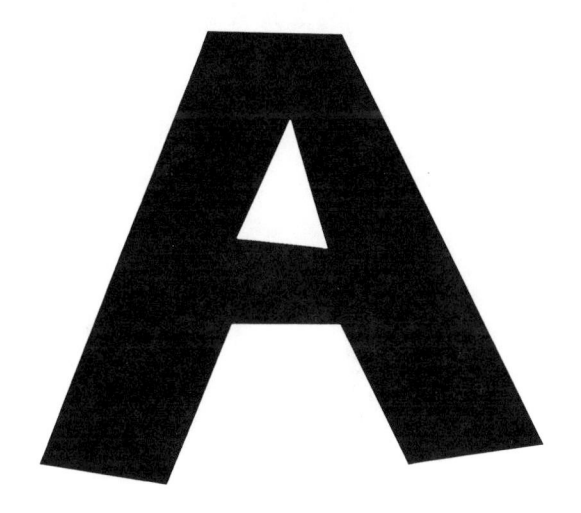

For the people who think that "computer design" must have a mechanical look, I offer this page. To achieve the hand-lettered look, I did the "A" using the straight line drawing tool in FreeHand. The letter is actually a series of straight lines. By using this technique, you can create a lot of unusual designs on the computer.

To get another "hand drawn" look, I used the FreeHand freehand tool. (That's not a typo; it's the correct way to describe it.) Then, the letters were filled in with a shade of grey while the outlines were left black.

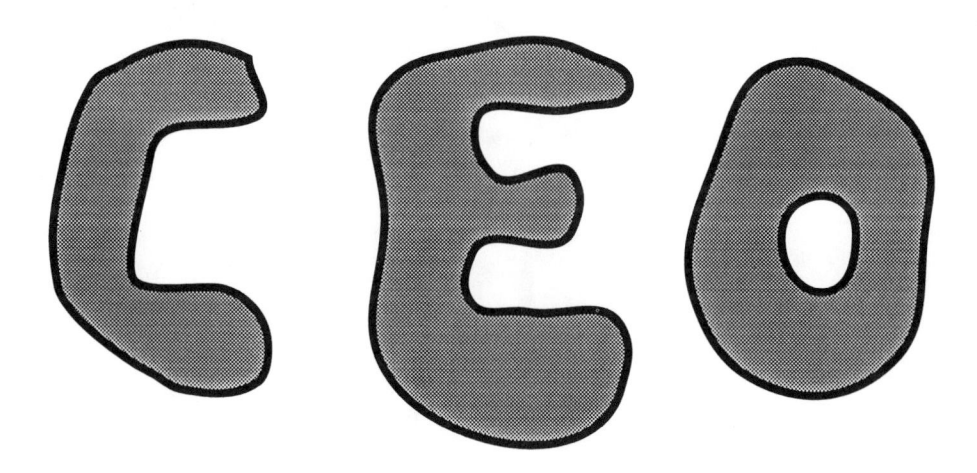

Illustration as Logo

If you want to create an illustration as a logo, the results can be outstanding. However, doing quality illustration on the computer is difficult for beginners.

The design at right is actually a package design for a Macintosh program, but it gives you an idea of the high level of design and illustration possible on the computer.

I included the lower design to show you that computer illustration doesn't have to look formal or rigid.

Both pieces were done by Clement Mok Designs, Inc., of San Francisco, one of the top firms in the field.

Art and Type Merged

First, Africa was set in Helvetica Black type. Then, the word was ungrouped, and the "A" was changed into a flat-topped triangle. Then, the Kudu head was simply put in place to finish the design.

This design started with Clearface Bold type, which was then skewed to give it the right angle for an italic look. The two giraffe heads were put in where the "F" letters would normally go.

Animal Based

The paw print, an element from Logo SuperPower, was simply copied and pasted on top of the circle. The type was added, and a nice school logo was completed in a couple of minutes.

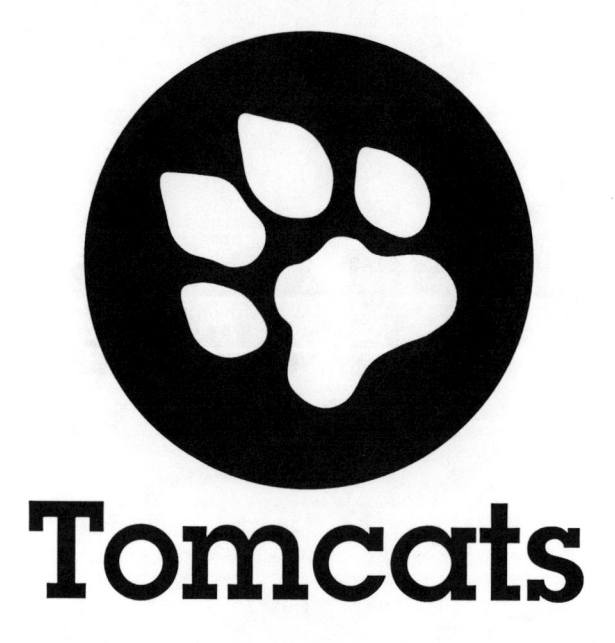

Tomcats

All the elements in this logo (except the type) are in Logo SuperPower. The medical cross is the base object, and the dog and cat elements were simply cut and pasted on to complete the design.

Dog & Cat Hospital

148

Shape inside a Shape

This design is actually just five circles, placed in an eye-catching configuration.

The diamond base object is the background for a set of seven circles, each getting progressively smaller as they go to the bottom of the design. This accurate progressive sizing of the circles was done using the "blend" feature of Freehand.

Overlapping Letters

The Putnam logo started in FreeHand with Helvetica Black type. The type was ungrouped, and the "line" was changed to 3 points - white. Then, the letters were simply moved to overlap each other.

Putnam

I started this design with the "9" as the base object. Then, "th" was placed in the white area of the number. The word "Annual" was set in type and converted to artwork. The "fill" was left black, and the "line" was changed to white to show the outline effect.

3-Dimensional Name

This eye-catching effect was created very simply: I set the word "TOP" and then copied it. The copy was changed to white, and then moved slightly to give the shadow effect you see here.

TOP

This interesting look requires no special work, and can even be done in PageMaker. To do this design, the type specification was simply "shadow" effect.

Chippy's

Back Shadow

This design began with the triangle on the right. Then, I copied it, reduced it, and moved the copy. It became the triangle at bottom left. Finally, I drew a single white line at the left of the original triangle. The line was cloned and moved, and the process was repeated to finish the design.

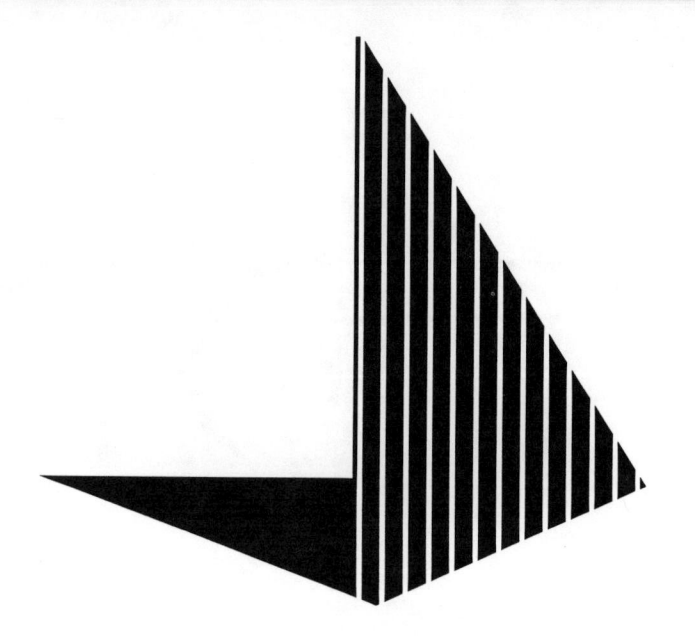

This interesting look is simply a base (round corner rectangle) with a white effect on top. The effect is actually made up of two pieces: a triangle and an oval. Since both are white, there is no indication that it's not a single drawing.

Stars & Stripes

The management of an Air Force base credit union wanted a design that would emphasize their connection to the sky — and to space. Their old logo had a rounded square shape, so I retained that equity in the base object. Next, I put the star in the upper right corner and added the twisting lines to complete the job.

This nice design was done in two segments: the top two lines are identical to the bottom two. To start, I made a long rectangular box, then added "curve points" to it. I then made the box into a curved shape, cut it in two pieces and dropped the right side to a lower position. Then I grouped the two pieces together. (You can see this finished piece as the top line.) I then copied the element and shrunk it to half its original height, while keeping its full length. Once the top two elements were done, I grouped them copied both and moved the copy to the bottom to finish the design.

Celestial

After I had placed the star on screen, I simply drew one effect: a curving triangle that was nearly horizontal. You can see it as the top one of the three white elements. Once it was complete and in place, I copied it, changed its shape slightly and moved it. I repeated the step to complete the bottom effect and the logo.

All the smaller ovals here are derived from the larger original, which forms the outside of the design. Each inside oval was simply reduced in size from the original.

To create the first oval, it was necessary to draw two concentric ovals, then move the inner one higher to align with the outer one. Then, the two elements were joined and filled with black, then grouped.

Diagonal Stripes

The base object for this design consisted of first setting the word "PACE" in type. Next, the letter "P" was converted to artwork and ungrouped. I then moved the left edge of the letter much farther left to create the black background I desired. To finish the logo, I drew the first white line at left, then cloned and moved it several times.

Once the black letter was on screen, I simply drew the first white line at the top of the design. It was cloned and moved, and the process was duplicated several times until I had the design I wanted.

Letter Blocks

Each letter here consists of two steps: making the black background, then placing the single white letter on top. The final position was done by using the "alignment" tool of FreeHand.

This design was done in a similar way to the one above. Except here, the size of the letter and block were planned to create the appearance of the white type flowing off the black foundation.

Circle Base with Type

First the circle; then the type. And then a white line, cloned and moved, then duplicated several times. Nice design in a couple of minutes.

The letter "a" was set in white on the black circle base object. Next, the letter was changed to artwork by the "convert to paths" feature of FreeHand. The letter was then copied and changed so that only the white outline remained. That outline was then copied and placed into position several times to complete the logo.

Circle Base - Abstract

This interesting design is actually composed of just two components: the circle and a simple angular white design which was cloned and moved several times to create the left half of the logo. Then, that half was grouped, copied and flipped to create the right half.

This is another logo that was done with the "blend" feature of FreeHand. Once the circle was done, I drew the top white design element. Then, I copied it and modified it, creating the bottom white element. Finally, I "blended" between the two to add the three middle design elements.

Circle Base - Object as Effect

The straight line tool of FreeHand was used to create the white part of this design. It was almost as simple as a "connect the dots" drawing. But when the background was changed to white on a black circle, it suddenly becomes a striking graphic.

This is a design which I did as part of a name change project for a client. Their new headquarters building has these beautiful "Old South" columns in front, and they wanted to somehow use that in the logo. I talked them out of using the building as such, and showed them this graphic as my first proposal. They bought it. Good choice.

Kentucky
Bank & Trust

Reverse Line Images

The "reverse" in this instance refers to using white lines in contrast with similar black lines. In this logo, each black line has a thinner white line sitting directly on top. When the effects are placed on the crescent base object, it creates an interesting graphic.

The eagle head base object was modified by two sets of lines: the reverse white lines at the top of the head, and the black lines extending from the lower portion of the design. Note: in order to get the exactly correct flow of the white lines, I simply used a copy of the top line of the eagle's head and made a number of duplicates.

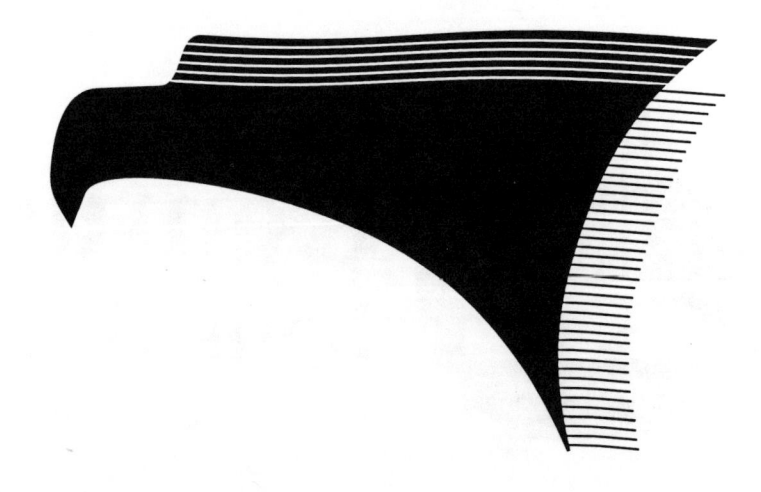

Multiple Images

To do any design like this, you first draw one of the elements. I started with the black one at the bottom. Next, I copied it and flipped it to have a mirror image next to the original piece. I then made 3 additional duplicates, which were "copied and rotated" in FreeHand. The final step was to change all but one element to grey.

This started off as four rows of five circles each. I turned it into an interesting design simply by changing some of the circles from black to grey.

161

Simulated Animation

The base object for this design is the black airplane. The next step I took was to use the straight line tool to create the first line of " shock waves" behind the plane. Then, by simply cloning and moving the line several times, the logo was done.

Once the star was on screen, I copied it and changed its fill to white. To complete the logo, I copied and reduced the star outline several times, moving each one to the back as the image got smaller.

Abstract with Initial

The base object "M" was magically transformed into a nice logo by the addition of three "ribbon" lines placed on top in white. Each of the three is the same design, simply a copy of the original.

Here's a different variation of "abstract with initial." This time, the abstract is the base object, while the initial is used as a graphic effect.

163

Object with Type

Quick design: I used the hanger from Logo SuperPower, then simply set the name in type. I covered the bottom part of the hanger with white before placing the name in front. Nice design for a small store.

The top of the "clapper" and its bottom are actually the same design. I began by making the bottom piece, then cloned it and flipped it. Next, I rotated the top piece into the proper position. Finally, I added the type.

Circular Type - Object Inside

Both the logos shown on this page were created using a Macintosh program called TypeStyler. The program has a visual selector that shows a sample of the output in advance. You can then use your favorite type face and have the design rendered on screen quickly.

Once each of these types was done in TypeStyler, I simply added an appropriate visual graphic inside the circle of type.

Type as Object

Once the "N" was on screen, I changed it to art, then skewed it to the desired slant. I added the first white element, then cloned and moved it several times to finish the design.

The base object "R" was set in type, then converted to art. Then, the white portion of the letter was removed, and the lower right "leg" was changed so that it descended below the base line. Next, I drew one of the white elements with the straight line tool, then copied it to finish the logo.

Type Duplicated

To get this look, I set the word "Dimension" in Helvetica Black type. Next, I copied the word twice. Then, I changed the first copy to standard Helvetica and changed the second copy to Helvetica Light. I changed each of the copies to a different shade of grey. Finally, I positioned the three pieces of type into place in order to create the dimensional effect.

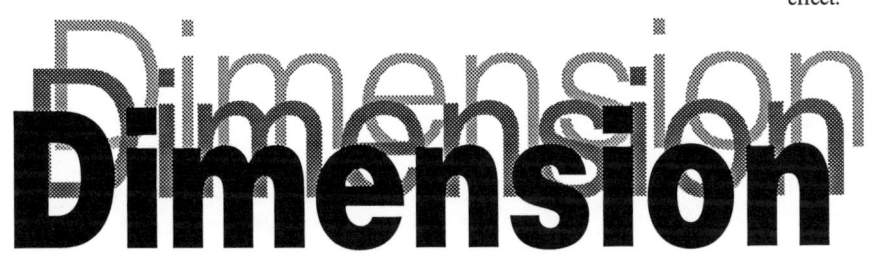

Dimension

This started simply enough, with "Jakarta" set in type. Then, I set the letter "J" as a separate piece of type and copied it four times. Then I aligned each "J" with the name and changed each one to a different shade of grey.

JJJJakarta

167

Object Duplicated

This design began with a basic shape of a single "arrowhead," which could normally serve as the base object. However, the base was duplicated to make a row of five "arrowheads," which serves as the complete logo.

This drop (it could be oil, water, a chemical, or whatever) could easily be used as a base object. However, I duplicated it several times, and changed each copy to a different shade of grey to make a nice design.

Letter made from Abstracts

Creating a series of 12 lines to make an abstract "A" took a little pre-planning. (Is that redundant? Is there such a thing as *post*-planning?) The planning began with the outline of an "A" placed on screen. Then I created the first element — the bottom one. Next, I cloned and moved it upward to create 11 identical lines. Each time the clone was moved, it was aligned with the left side of the "A." Finally, I changed the right side of all those lines so that they aligned with the right side.

This logo began with a large white letter "P" outlined on screen on top of a black circle. Next, I drew the top white effect, copied it several times and moved each copy to align with the right outline of the "P." To finish, I deleted the outline of the "P." Since the white elements bleed off the left side of the circle, it was not necessary to make any other changes to have the desired visual effect.

Type Inside Abstract

Once I had drawn this base object, I set the type. Next, I copied the bottom line of the base object and used the FreeHand feature that lets you align type along an irregular line. Finally, I changed the curved type to white and put it into position.

Making this logo was simply a matter of converting the type to art, then extending the two type elements so that they extended beyond the edge of the base object.

Type Merges with Logo

Before you try using a circle object (such as these basketballs) for an "O," check your proposed type face. This design works well because the actual "O" letters would be perfectly round. Most fonts have oval-shaped "O" letters and this technique may not work as well in many of these types.

There might be a trickier way to do this effect with type, but my way is fast and sure. I drew the horse, then set all the black type. Then, I set the white "o" and "h" as separate pieces and put them in place. Note that the "h" has a shadow effect. I copied the white "h" and changed it to black, then placed it behind the white "h" offsetting it slightly to create the shadow line.

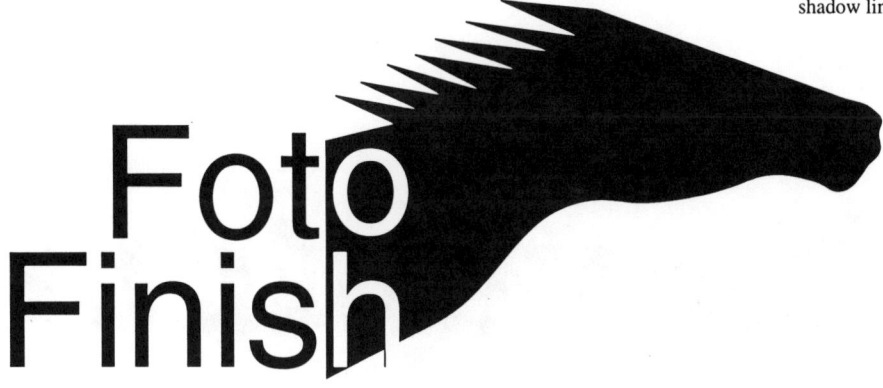

Type Changes Weight

This is a nice graphic concept that was very easy to do. The first two lines were both Helvetica Black. Then "12" had its line weight changed to 5 points to make it appear thicker. Then, the word "Diet" was set in Helvetica and "Club" was set in Helvetica Light.

12
Week
Diet
Club

The entire word "Momentum" was originally set in Helvetica Black. I changed the type to art (convert to paths) and each letter became an individual piece of art. To get the different "weights" for each letter, I simply changed the "line" specifications. The "M" has an 8 point black outline, while the final "m" has a 5 point white outline.

Momentum

Globe Based

World Travel

You could draw this design yourself by using circles and ovals, with a few straight lines to show the parallels of latitude. Add the black oval and you have a neat graphic.

Trans-Global

I began this logo by drawing a circle as a guideline. Next, I drew an 18-point line (slightly angled) in the center of the circle. Then, I cloned the line, moved it and repeated the step until I had reached the top of the circle. This left me with a set of lines all the same length. To make the lines fit into the circle, I changed each line's width so that it stopped at the edge of the circle. This completed the top half of the logo. Once that was done, I grouped the lines, cloned the group and flipped the image to make the bottom half of the globe.

Fake Embossing

To create the embossed look type, you need three identical copies of the words. The first one is to be the exact same color as your background. A second will be white type and the other will be type in a darker shade than the original.

The original (same color as the background) goes on top. The white type and the darker type go behind the background. Move the white type slightly northeast of the original type; move the darker type slightly southwest of the original.

You can create a similar effect using art instead of type, as shown at right.

Small Images Repeated

You can get some nice visuals by repeating a smaller image to create a logo. Here, the initial "L" is made from a chevron, and the result is a "tire tracks" logo.

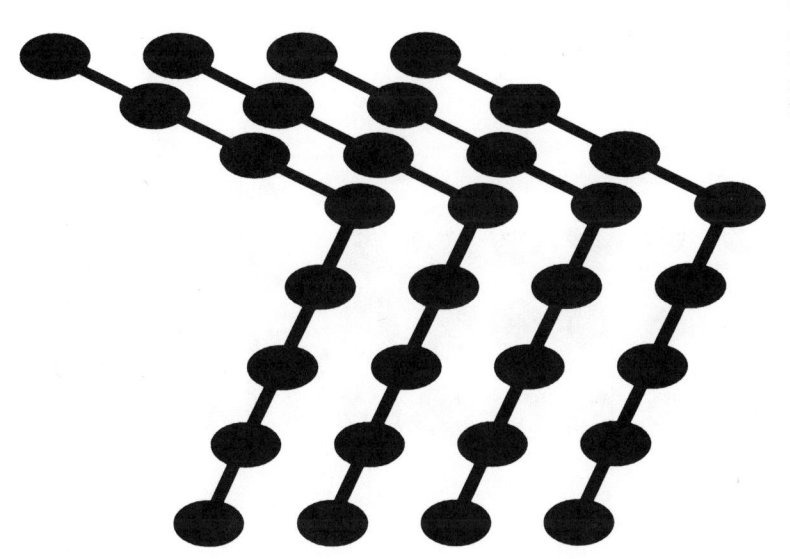

This logo is the result of simply combining ovals and straight lines. The arrangement of the multiple elements is what makes the design eye catching.

Halftone Dots

Let's look at this design one line at a time. I started with the small circle at the very top of the graphic. Then, I created the large round cornered square at the bottom of that line. Using the "blend" feature of FreeHand, I made all the interlocking elements in between. The result was "grouped" into a single element, which I then copied 3 times and placed into final position.

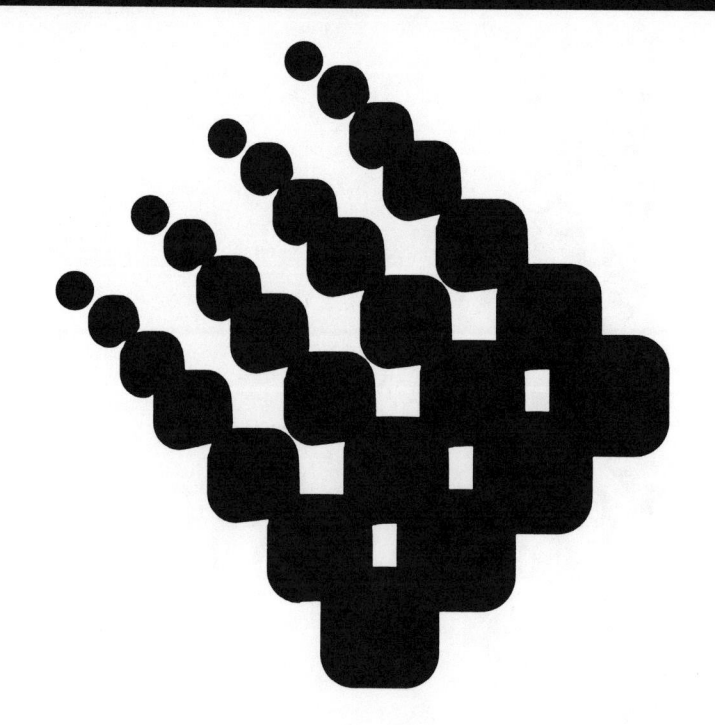

I started with the small circle at the top of the first line, then made the large circle at the end of the line (it was black when I started). I used the "blend" tool and the result was all the progressively larger circles. Then, I changed the big end circle to white. I grouped the whole line, copied it twice and added the "M" to finish the logo.

Pages & Paper

This began with a "D" set in Helvetica Black. The letter was changed to art, and the white portion in the center was eliminated. Finally, the white effect was drawn to resemble a page turning.

Dixon Paper

This design began with two thick straight lines (the book's covers). Then, I drew a circle and cut it in half to make the spine. Next, I added thin lines (for the pages) and to get the correct look, gave the edges a slightly curved alignment.

Darcie's Book Shop

Speed Lines

This design started off with a circle as the guideline. I then made the diamond shaped object that is the top element in the design. I kept repeating the diamond shape, elongating each new one as I worked downward, so that it was the same width as the circle each time. Once I reached the equator of the circle, I grouped all the diamonds, and copied and flipped the piece to create a circle full of very wide diamonds. Next, I added the thin speed lines at left, put the type on top and finally skewed the whole piece to add a feeling of motion.

This design is not nearly as complex to create as you might think at first. Actually, if you look closely at the top element, you'll see that it's not all that difficult to draw, and all the rest of the elements are duplicates of the top one. Once the first element was made, I simply cloned and moved it, repeating the stop to create the top half. Then, I grouped the design, copied it and flipped it to finish the bottom half.

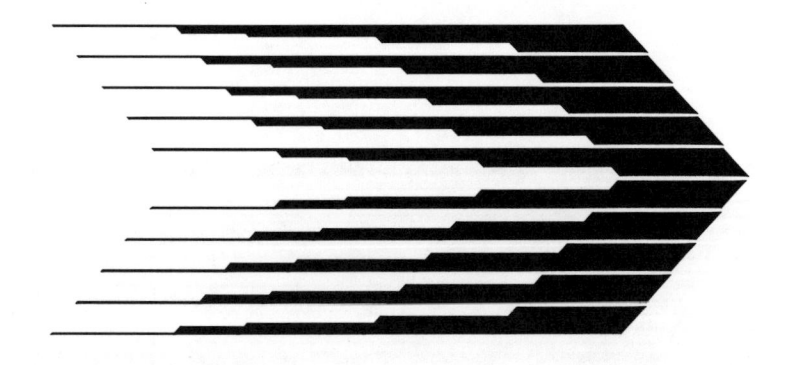

Pattern Background

Dottie's Fresh Pies

A patterned background may be as simple as a 20% screen with type on top.

Brick Masons, Inc.

Most drawing programs have a wide range of built-in patterns, such as the brick wall.

Repeat, Rotate & Add Object

To create this logo, I began with a circle drawn from the toolbox. Next, I drew one simple pointed object, cloned it and made it rotate around the perimeter of the circle to create the sunburst look. Finally, I placed the cactus in the center of the design.

The spiral effect was started with one of the segments drawn to the desired shape. Next, I cloned the element, and moved it 30 degrees around the center point. This step was repeated to create 12 identical effects. Finally, the arrow with a white line edge was placed on top of the entire piece.

Abstract with Meaning

THE BANGKOK CLUB

I got a fax one morning from our affiliate office in Bangkok. They wanted to see a couple of logos to present to The Bangkok Club, a very elite members-only group which occupies the top floors of a new office tower in the city. They sent me a photo of the building, which showed a beautiful structure with a 4-story penthouse (the club's quarters).

The top design is really a graphic representation of the top floors, while the bottom logo is an abstract of the building as a whole.

The Bangkok Club

Around the Corner

Both of the effects on this page were done using TypeStyler, although neither of the finished designs is on the "menu" of the program. Each logo was done by combining two different pieces of type.

The "corner" design was accomplished by using the "COR" and "NER" in matching (opposite) formats.

The "Upside Down" logo was done in a similar fashion. This piece required that the word "Down" be rotated 180 degrees.

Type with Partial Background

DONDE

This is a simple design that was done with a minimal amount of work, but the finished result shows just one way to add interest to an all-type design. (Consider using two colors to a design like this, and it really helps.) The grey box was drawn using the toolbox, and the type was placed on top. This basic concept has many possible variations. Try using various shapes, such as triangles, or even abstract shapes, and see what you get.

MARSHALL

This design began with a trapezoid being drawn from the toolbox. Next, the word "Marshall" was set in type and placed on top of the base. To get the shadow effect, the type was cloned, changed to white, and moved slightly to the lower right of the original type. To complete the design, the original "Marshall" black type was moved to the front of the white type.

183

Clone and Repeat/Shrink

Most drawing programs allow you to make a clone of a selected object, then reduce its size and move the cloned object to a designated location. This example of that technique was done with the bottom white effect as the starting point. To produce the logo, the original effect was cloned, shrunk to 95%, and moved 10 degrees. By "duplicating the move" a number of times, the white effects were done simply and accurately. The final look was done by putting the white elements on a black oval background.

This design was done using a similar technique to the one above. I started with the top design, then cloned it. Then I reduced it and moved it below the original. Using the "duplicate move" command several times, I did the design which you see here in seconds.

Letterspaced Name

The letters were set as five individual pieces, and the design used the automatic spacing feature in FreeHand to put the letters in their proper position. The diamonds in between were done the same way. Finally, the bottom line of diamonds was made by putting one into place and creating the series with the "clone, move and duplicate" features.

·R·O·V·E·R·

◆ ◆ ◆ ◆ ◆ ◆ ◆ ◆ ◆ ◆ ◆ ◆ ◆ ◆ ◆

In creating this design, each of the three lines was a separate block of copy, each with its own size specifications. Once they were in place, positioning was done with the automatic alignment feature of FreeHand.

E

Y E

E X A M

Letter in Various Sizes

This bold design was done by simply creating four separate blocks of copy — one for each letter. The letters were each sized to the correct proportion, and they were then placed in proper alignment to create the desired effect.

ALTA

This logo was planned to emphasize the pronunciation of the name: *de WITT*. To create a visual which would accomplish this, I set all the type in Helvetica Black Italic. To get the different weights from the same font, I changed the "line weight" specs of the letters "De" from "1 point black" to" 3 points white." This simple change made the difference in the weight of the letters.

DeWitt

Neon

The two designs on this page were done using a simple technique. Before we start, note that the word "NEON" was not done with type. Start each letter by drawing a single, fat line (these were 20 points) with round ends and joints. Color each line black (or a bright color). Next, clone the line. Change the clone's weight to "0" and change its color to white. Next, select the two end points and use the blend tool. I used 30 steps for these examples. Each letter is a separate piece of art, so you'll have to repeat this for each one.

Note that all the letters have the highlight slightly off center. It adds a nice touch, but be careful to do it right, or you'll end up with a "burned out" effect like the center stroke of the E.

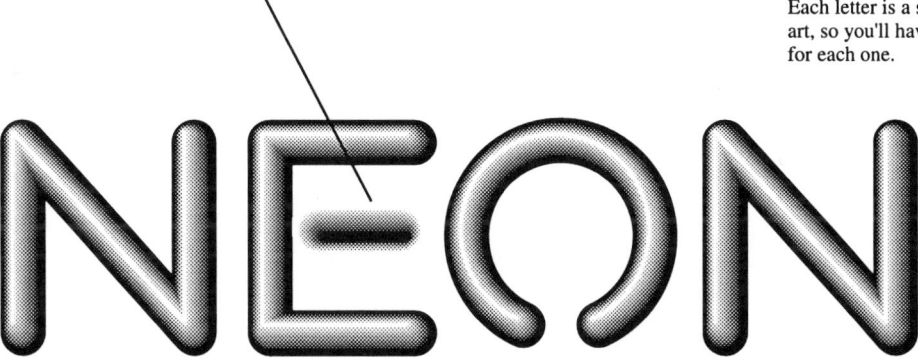

You may want to experiment with different weight, steps and colors. I learned how to do this from Before & After, a great publication described on page 108.

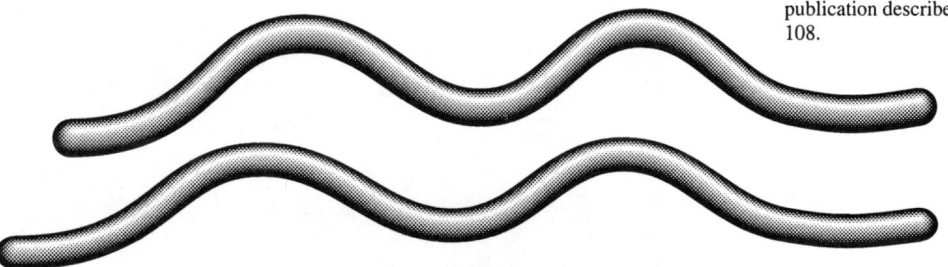

Glow Worms
Artificial Bait

187

Name in Rectangle - Off Center

This simple, bold logo was done by using the toolbox to create the black background. Then, the name "Aplha" was set in white type. For design effect, the lower case "p" extends beyond the edge of the black box.

Alpha

A nice design for a retail store was created with a rectangular box as the base object. Next, the name was set in lower-case type (with the word "shop" placed on a vertical plane to the rest of the words). Finally, a series of thin diagonal lines was placed on the upper left corner to give the design an overall balance.

the thoroughbred shop

Optical Illusion - Type

DOUBLETROUBLE

Both the effects on this page were made using TypeStyler. One unique feature of this program is its menu-driven operation which lets you learn how to use it very quickly.

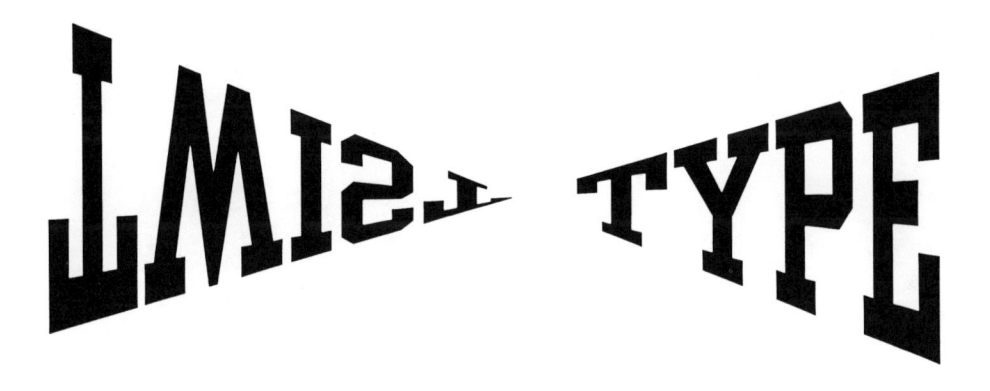

TWIST-TYPE

Part 3 - Software You'll Want

This section includes a number of programs which are of great help in the logo design process. With the exception of the PC programs listed here, I have them all, and find that they enhance your creativity and speed up the design process greatly.

Each application listed is accompanied by my brief description of what the program does, as well as some examples of the output. For your convenience, each program listed has an address and phone number in case you want to order or get additional information. For your convenience, they are designated with an Apple or PC to show their availability in the different platforms. PC

Add-Depth

Add-Depth is a program that automatically adds depth and perspective to type and line art. The program is easy to learn and simple to operate, yet it lets you create some very detailed comprehensive samples of package designs, as well as three-dimensional type and shapes. The program allows you to import two-dimensional objects created in Illustrator or FreeHand (such as the deer below) and then add dimensional effects.

addDepth is a product of Ray Dream, Inc. 1804 N. Shoreline, Mountain View, CA 94043. Phone (415) 960-0767.

Adobe Dimensions

Adobe Dimensions automatically generates shading based on lighting, view angles and surface properties which you select. You can get a 3-D look with type, line objects, or graphics drawn in programs such as Illustrator, FreeHand or Canvas. The program also allows the rendering of mock-ups for package designs, etc.

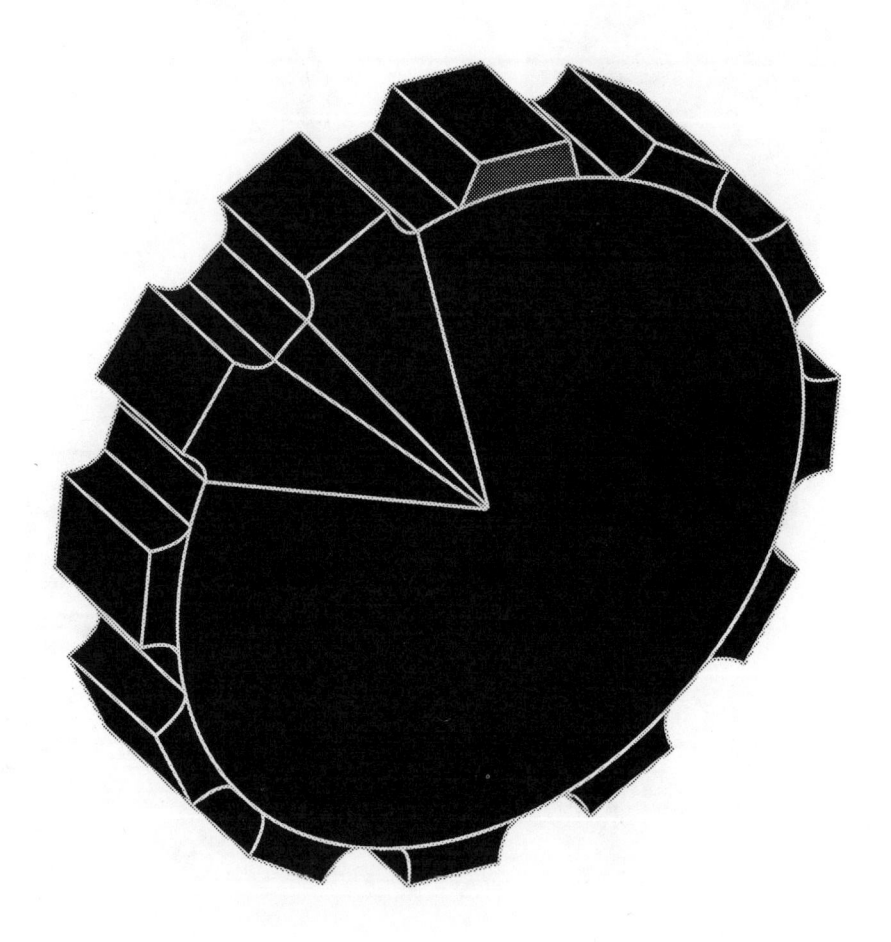

Adobe Dimensions is a product of Adobe Systems, 1585 Charleston Rd. PO Box 7900, Mountain View, CA 94039. Phone (800) 833-6687 or (415) 961-4400.

Adobe Multiple Master Fonts

To someone who is serious about using type, Adobe's Multiple Master Fonts are a giant step forward. (In my opinion, whoever came up with this concept is the Gutenberg of the late 20th Century.) Simply put, one basic type face can be altered to create 28,000 different varieties of the same font. On this spread, you see just a few examples of the Myriad font. When I try any new program, I have a rule of thumb: If you can read only a few pages of the manual and make it function properly in less than five minutes, it's "user friendly." This major breakthrough is definitely in that category.

Myriad

Myriad

Myriad

Myriad

Myriad

Myriad

Myriad

Myriad

Myriad

Myriad

Myriad

Myriad

Myriad Ital. *__Myriad Ital.__*

Myriad Ital. *__Myriad Ital.__*

Myriad Ital. *__Myriad Ital.__*

Myriad Ital. *__Myriad Ital.__*

__Myriad Ital.__ *__Myriad Ital.__*

__Myriad Ital.__ *__Myriad Ital.__*

 Adobe Multiple Master Fonts are products of Adobe Systems, 1585 Charleston Rd. PO Box 7900, Mountain View, CA 94039. Phone (800) 833-6687 or (415) 961-4400.

Adobe Multiple Master Fonts

When Adobe first introduced Multiple Master Fonts, they came up with two faces: Myriad (previous pages) and Minion, which is shown on this spread. As of this book's press deadline, they were the only two faces available. I repeat my thoughts from the previous spread: any designer who is serious about type will find that this is a major addition to your computer bag of tricks.

Minion

Minion

Minion

Minion

Minion

Minion

Minion

Minion

Minion Italic

Minion Italic

Minion Italic

Minion Italic

Minion Italic

Minion Italic

Minion Italic

 Adobe Multiple Master Fonts are products of Adobe Systems, 1585 Charleston Rd. PO Box 7900, Mountain View, CA 94039. Phone (800) 833-6687 or (415) 961-4400.

Altsys Fontographer

Altsys Fontographer gives you the power to create your own fonts or modify existing fonts. For the professional designer who is serious about corporate identity, this is an excellent tool that will allow a great deal of creative freedom. Yet, it is quickly learned and the novice can also use this for enhancing logo designs and corporate identity programs.

ANDES

ANDES

ANDES

Altsys Fontographer is a product of Altsys Corporation, 269 Renner Road, Richardson, TX. Phone (214) 680-2060.

Bitstream Makeup

Bitstream MakeUp is a PC-only program that lets you quickly manipulate words and letters to create effects like these shown here. The program gives the PC user an additional tool for creating unusual graphics.

HAPPY BIRTHDAY

AROUND TOWN

GROWING

NEWSLETTER

PC **Bitstream MakeUp** is a product of Bitstream, Inc., 215 First Street, Cambridge, MA. 02142   Phone (800) 522-3668.

Effects Specialist

Effects Specialist is a program that has something for everyone, although many of the best effects have very limited use. For creating logos, this program is best when it is used to produce only one or two letters, since some of the results can be very busy for longer words.

Cookie Cutter

Pyramid

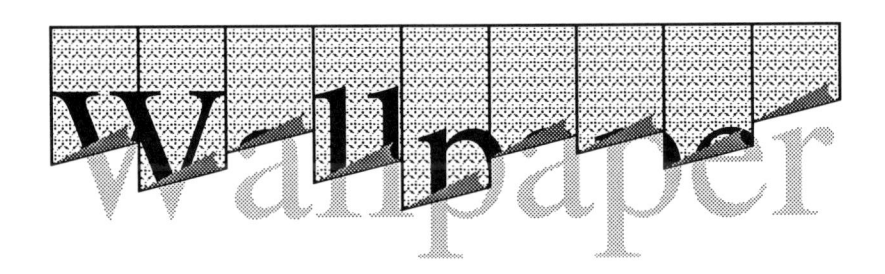

Effects Specialist is a product of Postcraft International Inc., 27811 Avenue Hopkins, Suite 6, Valencia, CA 91355. Phone (805) 257-1797.

FontMonger

FontMonger adds value to your existing font collection by letting you convert and customize your outline fonts. For example you can convert all your TrueType fonts to Postscript format to have a standard system.

In addition, you can use FontMonger to design an entirely new font. You can also import a logo into a font, so that it is produced with single keystroke and is part of your typeset paragraph. The program also lets you merge characters from several fonts into a single font, add unusual fractions, and even export type characters for modification in graphics programs.

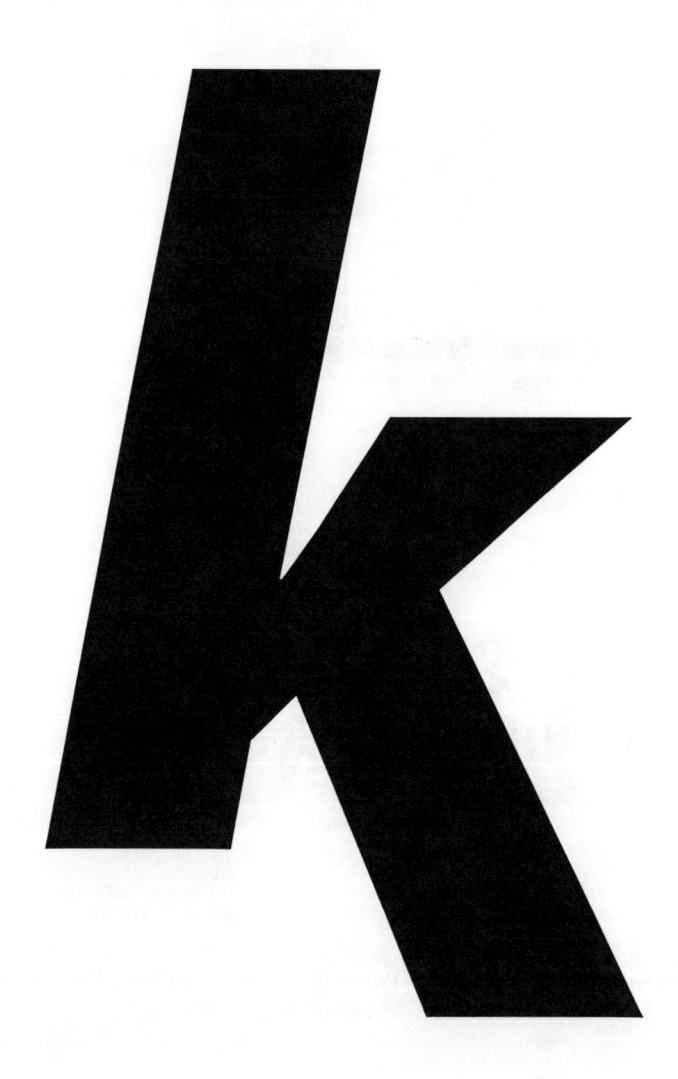

R R

Your logo goes here

 FontMonger is a product of Ares Software, P. O. Box 4667, 561 Pilgrim Drive, Suite D, Foster City, CA. Phone (415) 578-9090.

Font Studio

      Letraset's Font Studio is a very powerful program that lets you create new type fonts. It is a highly effective tool for use in creating customized fonts, which many firms desire for their corporate identity. The program's ability to store fragments of individual characters makes it a snap to create a consistent alphabet. Font Studio can also import Illustrator 1.1 files or use TIFF and PICT files as templates. While this program has so many features, it does take some time to learn.

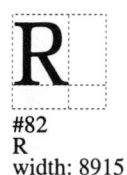

left sidebearing: 340
right sidebearing: 57
top: 10060
bottom: 0

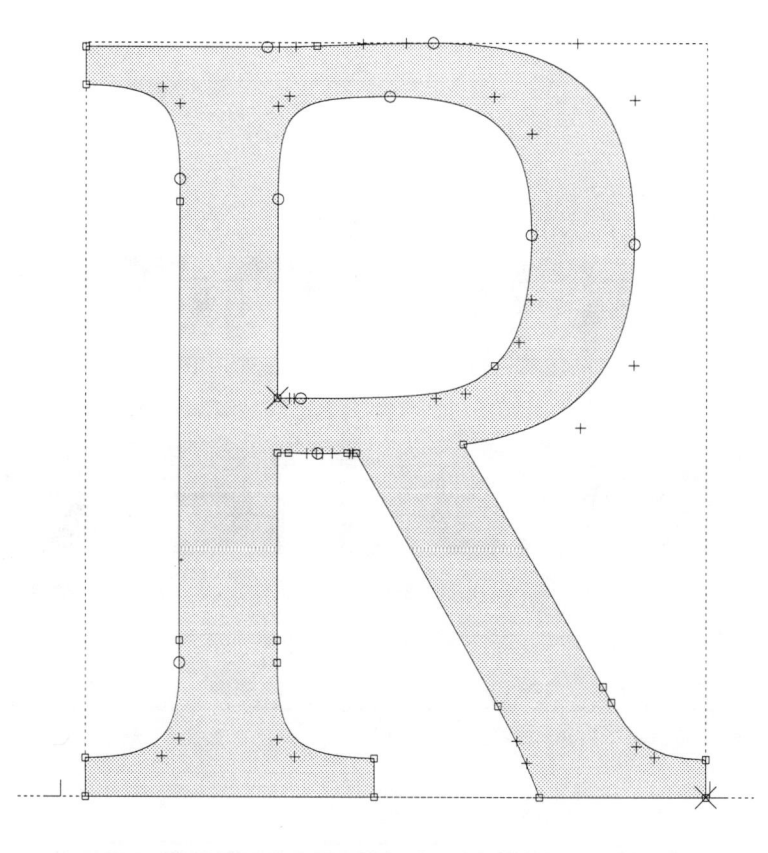

#82
R
width: 8915

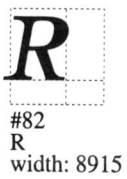

R
#82
R
width: 8915

left sidebearing: -1126
right sidebearing: -462
top: 10027
bottom: 0

R

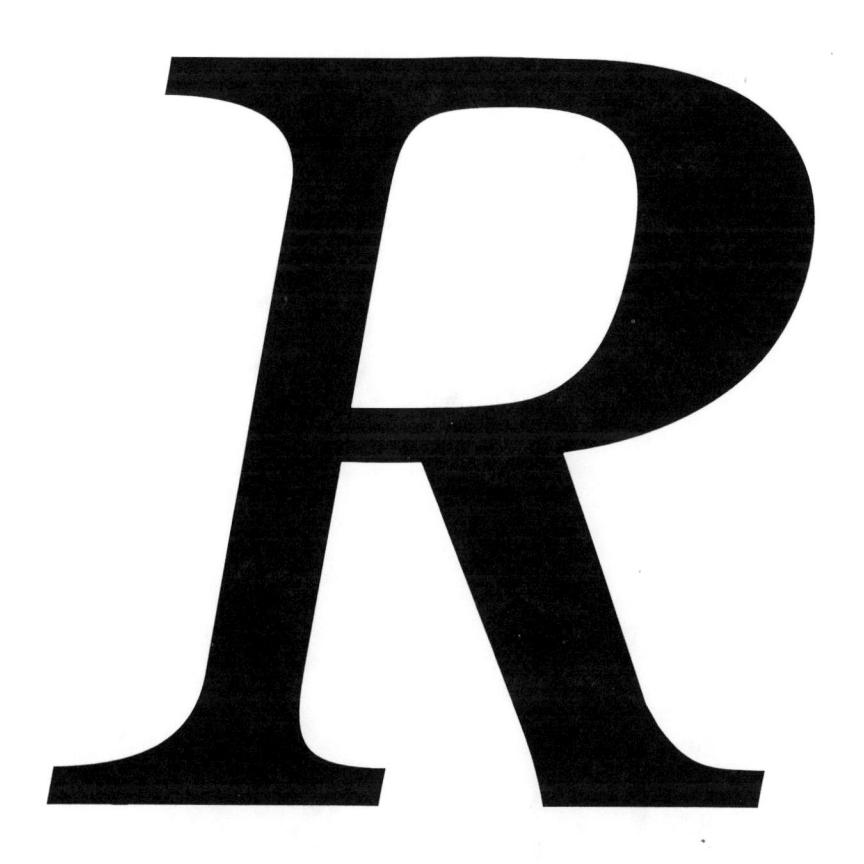

 FontStudio is a product of Letraset USA, Inc., 40 Eisenhower Drive, Paramus, NJ. Phone (800) 343-8973 or (201) 845-6100.

Letra Studio

For creating unique distortion effects, Letra Studio provides a large variety of "envelopes" which allow the user to create some highly interesting type effects. In addition, the program allows the importing of Adobe Illustrator artwork, so it can also manipulate and change the shape of logo effects from other packages. The many possible shapes can all be changed and modified by use of Bezier controls. This is a highly recommended tool for anyone who wants to produce unusual graphics with type.

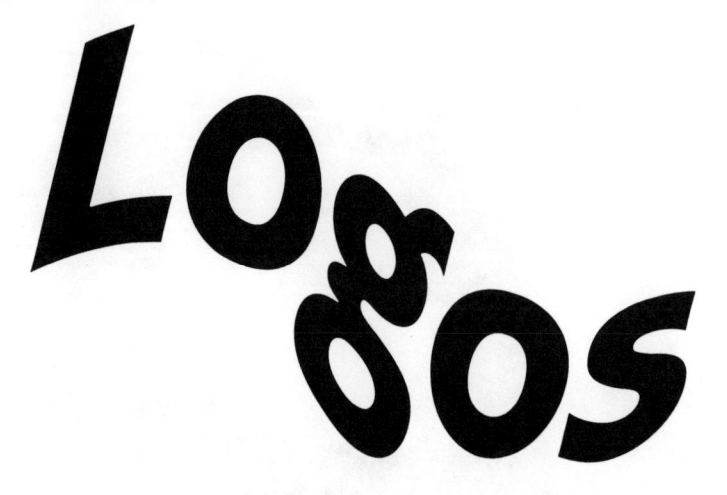

Logos

Graphics

Humbert

Merkins, Ltd.

 LetraStudio is a product of Letraset USA, Inc., 40 Eisenhower Drive, Paramus, NJ. Phone (800) 343-8973 or (201) 845-6100.

MenuFonts

Unlike the other programs discussed in this section, this application doesn't actually produce any graphics which show up on a printer. Yet, for the designer who is serious about type faces and their value in creating logos, this is a real time saver.

MenuFonts lets you see what a font looks like before you select while you are in your drawing or page layout program. The pull-down type menu displays the name of the font in its actual type face. In addition, icons on the font menu identify each font as TrueType, Postscript or Bitmapped.

The program menu automatically eliminates font prefixes (such as B, I, UL, etc.) so all your fonts will be in alphabetical order. You also preview various font sizes on screen, so you don't have to experiment so much to find the size you have in mind.

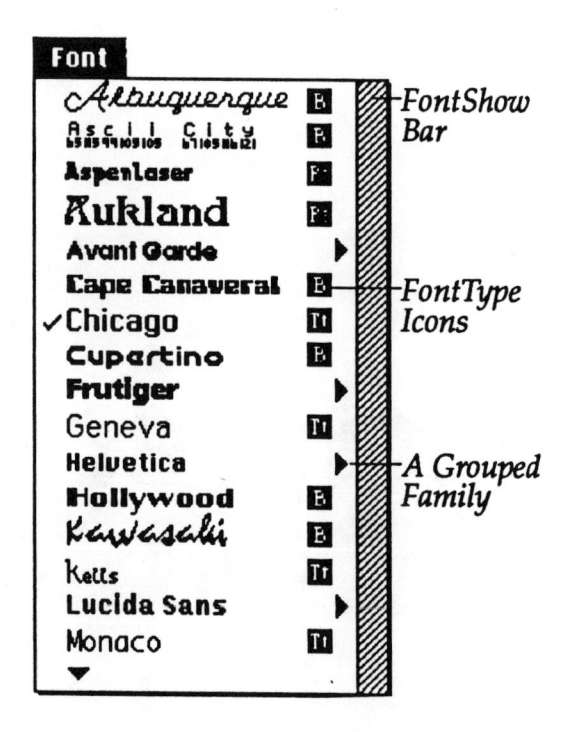

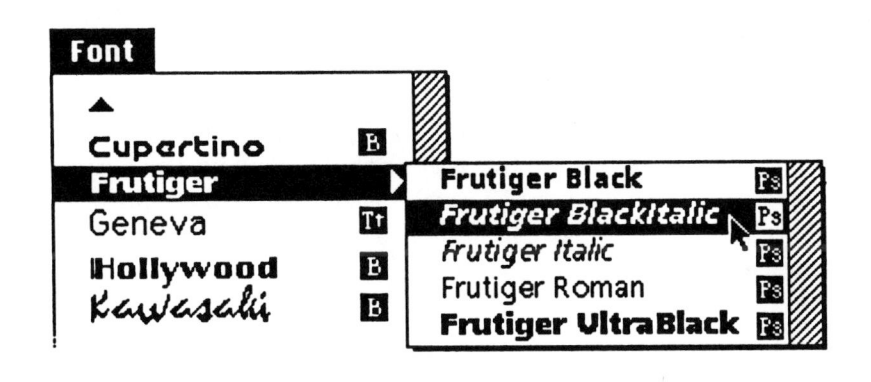

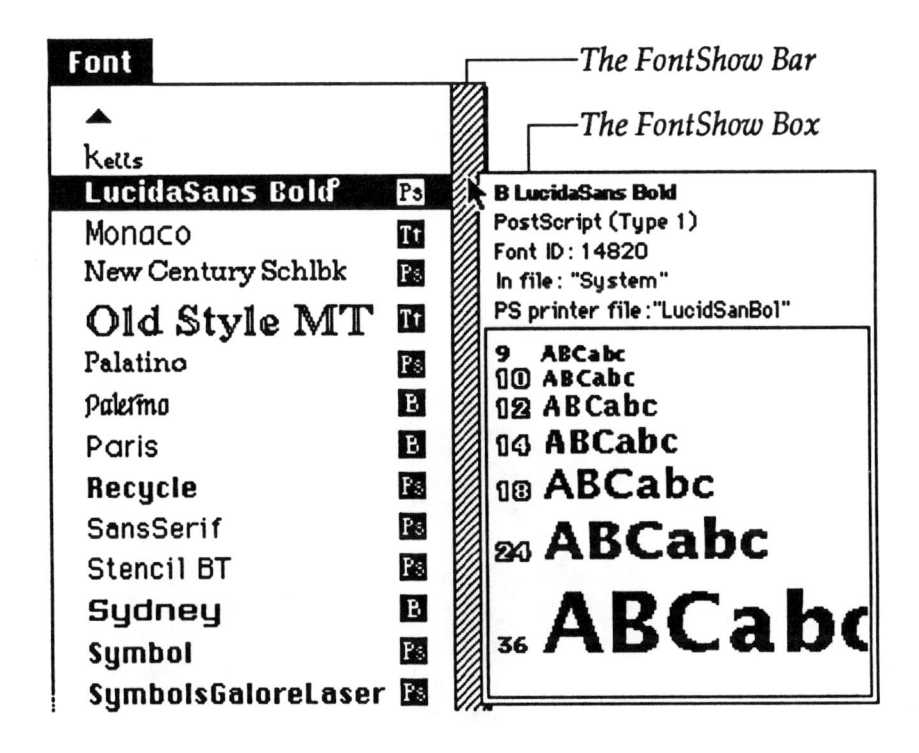

MenuFonts™ is a product of Dubl-Click Software, Inc., 22521 Styles Street, Woodland Hills, CA 91367-1730. Phone (800) 266-9525.

StrataType 3d

StrataType 3d is another of the new 3-dimensional graphic programs that lets you create dimensional type effects. This program lets you set type on a curve and draw your own bevels. There are 17 bevels already in the application for those who don't have the drawing skills needed to create their own. There are textures such as wood, brick, etc. and you can even scan in your own images to use in the program.

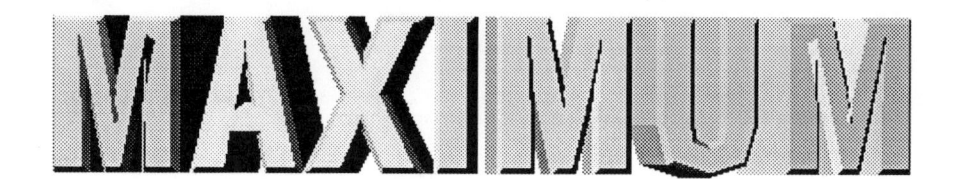

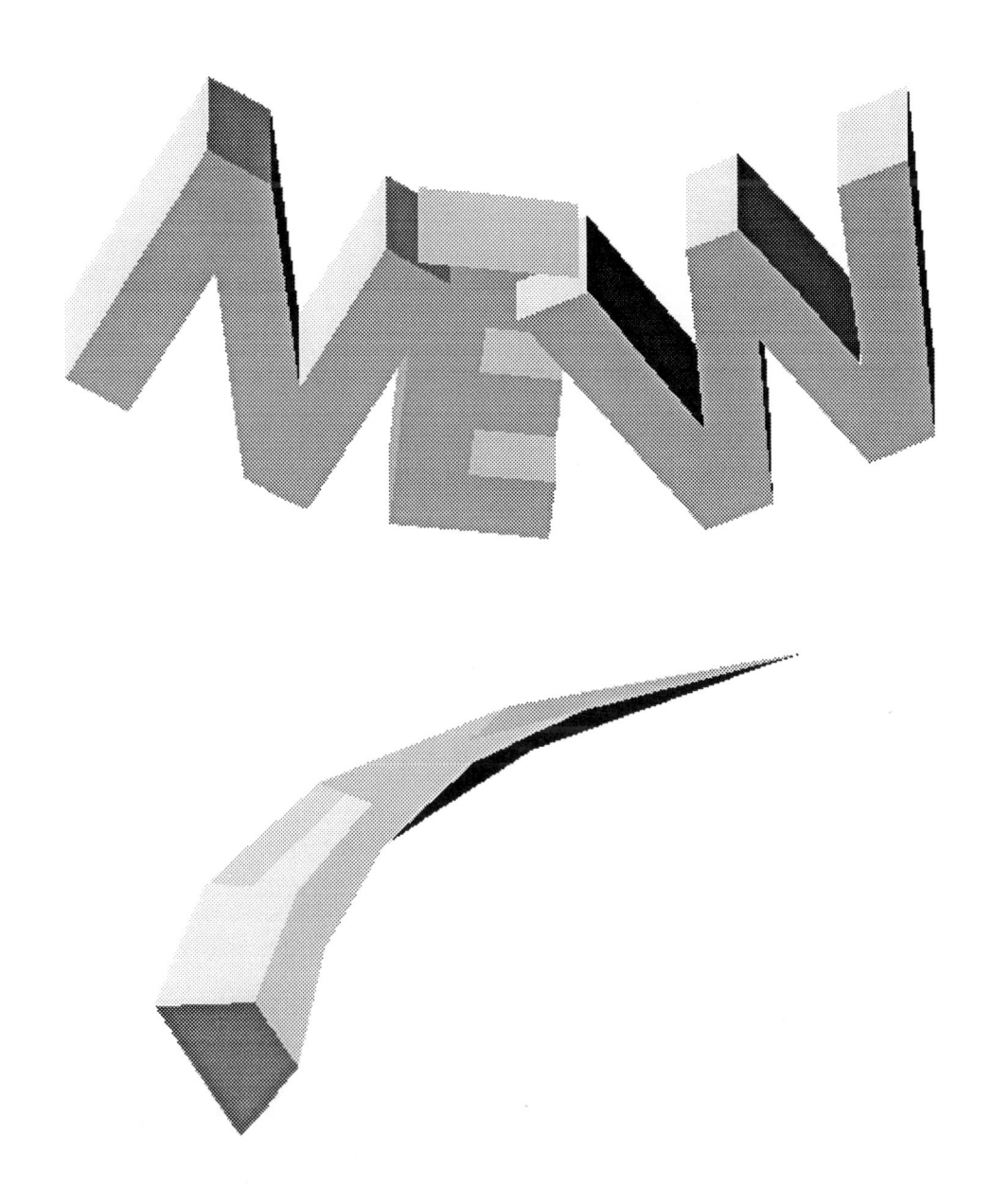

StrataType 3d is a product of Strata, Inc., 2 W. St. George Blvd. Ancestor Square, Suite 2100, St. George, UT 84770. Phone (801) 628-5218

The TypeBook

When you're producing a design system (see Chapter 11) you really need to have type spec sheets which show the various approved type fonts and how they appear in different sizes.

Garamond-Bold-DTC

6 pt. ABCDEFGHIJKLMNOPQRSTUVWXYZabcdefghijklmnopqrstuvwxyz0123456789!?,"¢$&%{}*
7 pt. ABCDEFGHIJKLMNOPQRSTUVWXYZabcdefghijklmnopqrstuvwxyz0123456789!?,"¢$&%{}*
8 pt. ABCDEFGHIJKLMNOPQRSTUVWXYZabcdefghijklmnopqrstuvwxyz0123456789!?,"¢$&%{}*
9 pt. ABCDEFGHIJKLMNOPQRSTUVWXYZabcdefghijklmnopqrstuvwxyz0123456789!?,"¢$&%{}*
10 pt. ABCDEFGHIJKLMNOPQRSTUVWXYZabcdefghijklmnopqrstuvwxyz0123456789!?,"¢$&%{}*
12 pt. ABCDEFGHIJKLMNOPQRSTUVWXYZabcdefghijklmnopqrstuvwxyz01234567
14 pt. ABCDEFGHIJKLMNOPQRSTUVWXYZabcdefghijklmnopqrstuvwxy
18 pt. ABCDEFGHIJKLMNOPQRSTUVWXYZabcdefghijklm

48 pt. **ABCDEFGHIJKLMN OPQRSTUVWXYZa bcdefghijklmnopq rstuvwxyz0123456 789!?,"¢$&%{}***

9/10
This page was generated by "theTypeBook". A freeware power tool from Jim Lewis. Customized versions are available in which the page footer is configured to your specifications. A typical layout would include a logo and company address information. Artwork is limited to a height of 32 pts. The combined width of both copy and artwork is limited to the printed area. The fee for customization is $45(US). To order contact Jim Lewis at the address shown below.

10/10
This page was generated by "theTypeBook". A freeware power tool from Jim Lewis. Customized versions are available in which the page footer is configured to your specifications. A typical layout would include a logo and company address information. Artwork is limited to a height of 32 pts. The combined width of both copy and artwork is limited to the printed area. The fee for customization is $45(US). To order contact Jim Lewis at the address sh

11/12
This page was generated by "theTypeBook". A freeware power tool from Jim Lewis. Customized versions are available in which the page footer is configured to your specifications. A typical layout would include a logo and company address information. Artwork is limited to a height of 32 pts. The combined width of both copy and artwork is limited to the pri

96 pt. **AaBbCcD**

theTypeBook
A Power Tool from Jim Lewis

Customized/Registered versions are available from
Golden State Graphics • 2137 Candis • Santa Ana, CA 92807
714/542-5518 • CIS 71650,2373 • AOL JimXLewis

The TypeBook fills this need very well, and is available free to Macintosh users when you send a postage-paid mailer and an 800K disk. A customized version with your logo (or whatever) is available for $45. The generic version is shown at left. A custom sample is below.

 The Type Book is a product of Golden State Graphics (Jim Lewis) 2137 Candis Avenue, Santa Ana, CA 9206. Phone (714) 542-5518.

TypeStyler

This is a very user-friendly program that lets you create a large variety of shapes with type. The system has Bezier curve controls that allow you a great deal of editing freedom. The type images created in TypeStyler can be exported and combined with images created in other programs. This is an easily-learned program that will greatly enhance the quality and variety of your design output.

SQUEEZE

DOUBLE CURVES

BOTTOM ARCH

ROUND AND ROUND

VERTICAL ARC

 TypeStyler is a product of Brøderbund Software, Inc. 500 Redwood Blvd., PO Box 6125, Novato, CA 94948 Phone (800) 521-6263 or (415) 382-4400.

TreacyFaces Typeface Collection

The TreacyFaces Typeface Collection is a highly original and unique library of fonts. Some are individual weight designs, and some are type families with as many as 16 weights for maximum flexibility. These fonts are regarded as some of the best available due to their superior drawing quality. They're also noted for their careful attention to kerning, with between 1700 and 4000 kerning pairs per typeface weight. This provides for nearly total automatic letterspacing that sets a new quality standard in keyboarded typography.

ONE OF A KIND!

TF Hôtelmoderne™
Created by
Treacyfaces,
in 1987-91.

TF Forever®
Created by
Treacyfaces,
1986-90.

Our love is Forever, my sweet! I swear it!

Send it by Air.

Why, this, here's called a Gazebo, sonny.

TF Habitat™ Condensed
Created by Treacyfaces, 1986–90.

TF Avian™
Created by Treacyfaces, 1991–92.

TF Akimbo™
Created by Treacyfaces, 1991–92.

ACROSS THE DANCE FLOOR WITH Legs akimbo!

TF Maltby™
Created by Treacyfaces, 1992.

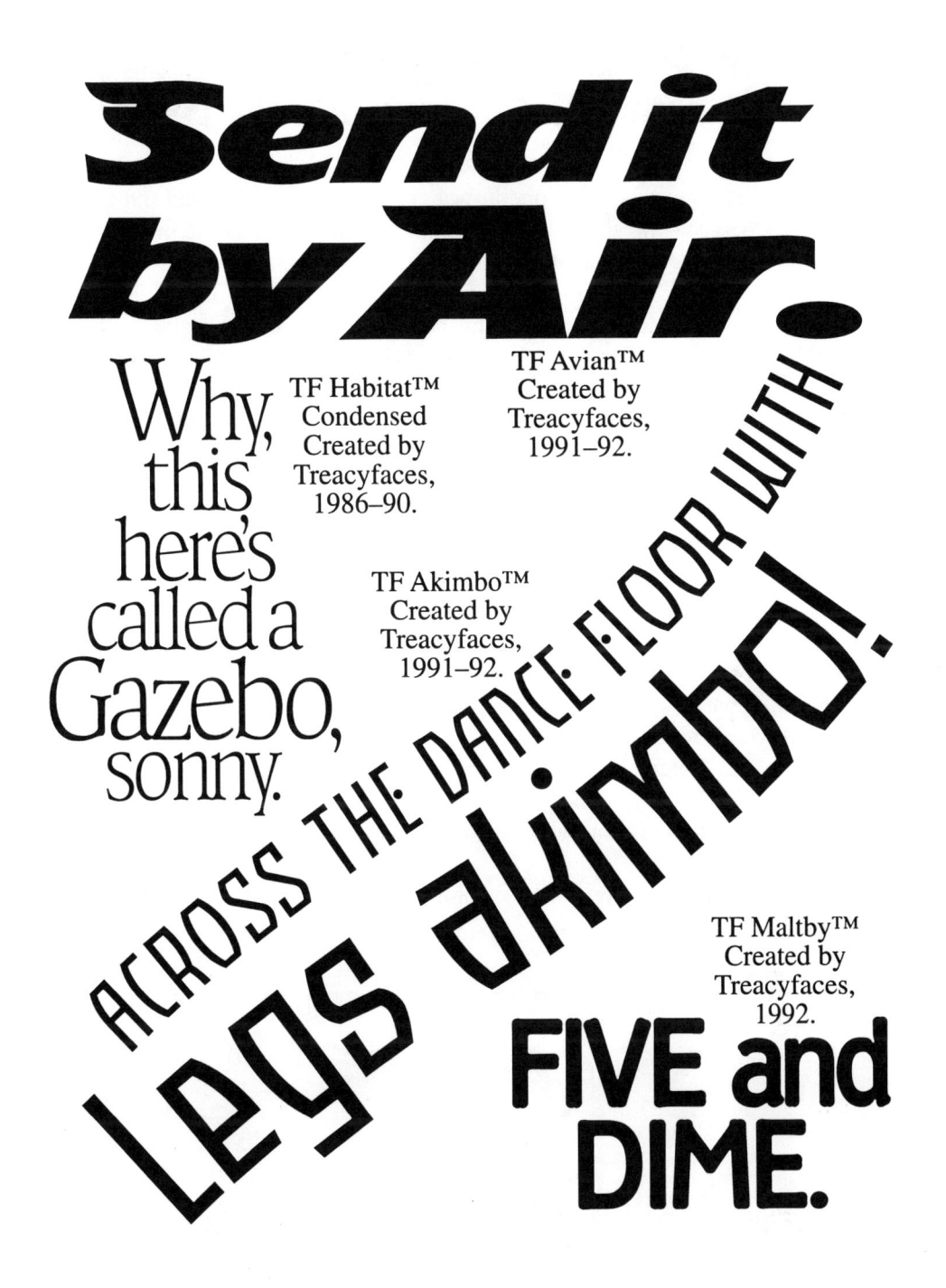

FIVE and DIME.

 TreacyFaces Typefaces Collection is a product of TreacyFaces, Inc., P.O. Box 26036, West Haven, CT 06516-8036. Phone (203) 389-7073.

221

Logo SuperPower

Just so you'll know -- Logo SuperPower is a product that I created shortly after I got my first Macintosh several years ago. I created this system because there was no program existing that specifically addressed logo design.

I'm giving it four pages in this book for two reasons: (1) it's really a terrific product. It helps you do world-class logos in literally minutes. (2) this section has about a dozen specialized products mentioned, and Logo SuperPower is just as good as any of the others. I'm sure not going to leave it out just to appear modest.

Thousands of people have bought Logo SuperPower and have turned their computer into a profit center. I highly recommend it (and not just because I created it.) Look how it works and I think you'll see why people like it so much.

Logo SuperPower® is a graphic database of more than 2,000 "design elements" that you can combine and manipulate in an infinite number of ways. For the Mac, FreeHand and Illustrator versions are available. For the PC platform, the design elements may be imported into programs such as Corel Draw, Arts & Letters, Micrografx Designer, FreeHand, Illustrator, and any other application which accepts AI EPS art files.

Here are just a few samples of the 2,000+ design elements in the Logo SuperPower system.

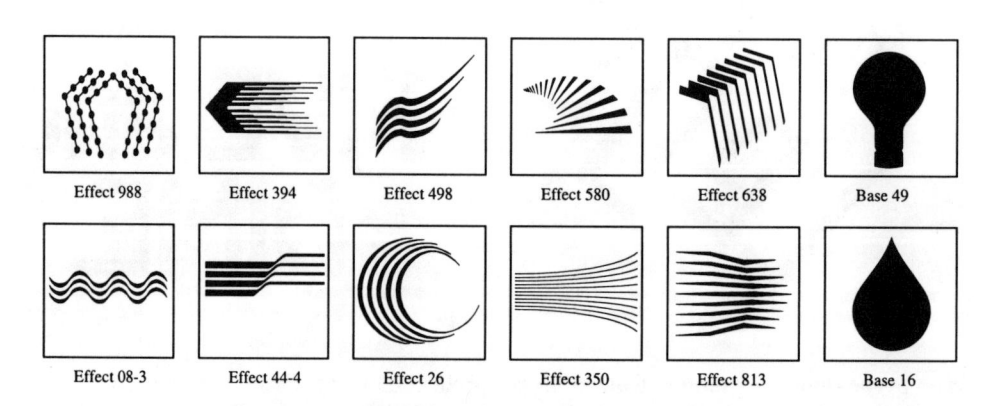

| Effect 988 | Effect 394 | Effect 498 | Effect 580 | Effect 638 | Base 49 |
| Effect 08-3 | Effect 44-4 | Effect 26 | Effect 350 | Effect 813 | Base 16 |

To use Logo SuperPower, you start with a fresh page in a drawing program, such as FreeHand, Illustrator, Corel Draw, etc. Then, you look through the instruction manual which shows all 2,000+ design elements and choose which of the Logo SuperPower elements you want to import to the page. As you can imagine, seeing all these pre-drawn design elements is a great idea starter, not to mention the fact that you don't have to spend any time actually drawing your design elements. Once you have the design element on screen, you can "ungroup" and make any changes you want. Below you will see step by step how some logos were created using Logo SuperPower. All were done on the Macintosh, using Aldus FreeHand. You can do similar quality work in Illustrator on the Mac, and in virtually any drawing program on the PC.

Three examples of logos done with Logo SuperPower®

Start with a circle from the toolbox.

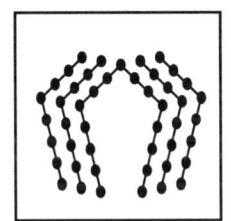

Logo SuperPower Effect 988 is used

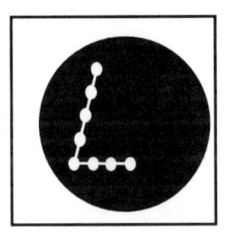

Use only part o the design element. Put it on the circle.

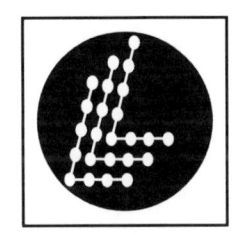

Duplicate the element twice to finish the job.

Start with Base 49, the light bulb.

Add effect 580. Change it to white.

Position the effect on top of the bulb, and change its shape.

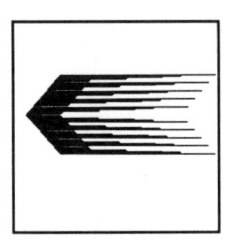

Begin with Effect 394.

Delete all but one part of the element. Rotate it.

Place a T on the Screen to be used as a guideline.

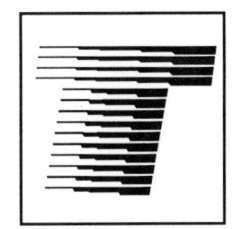

Place element at top of T; copy, change & move it several times. Delete T to finish.

223

Logo SuperPower

Logo SuperPower also has thirty templates such as those shown here which can be used to make presentations which show how logos will be utilized. All the other "application" samples shown in this book are done with Logo SuperPower templates.

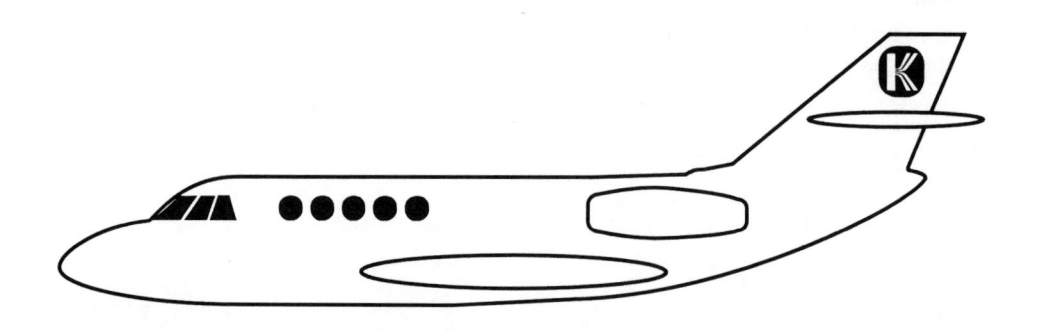

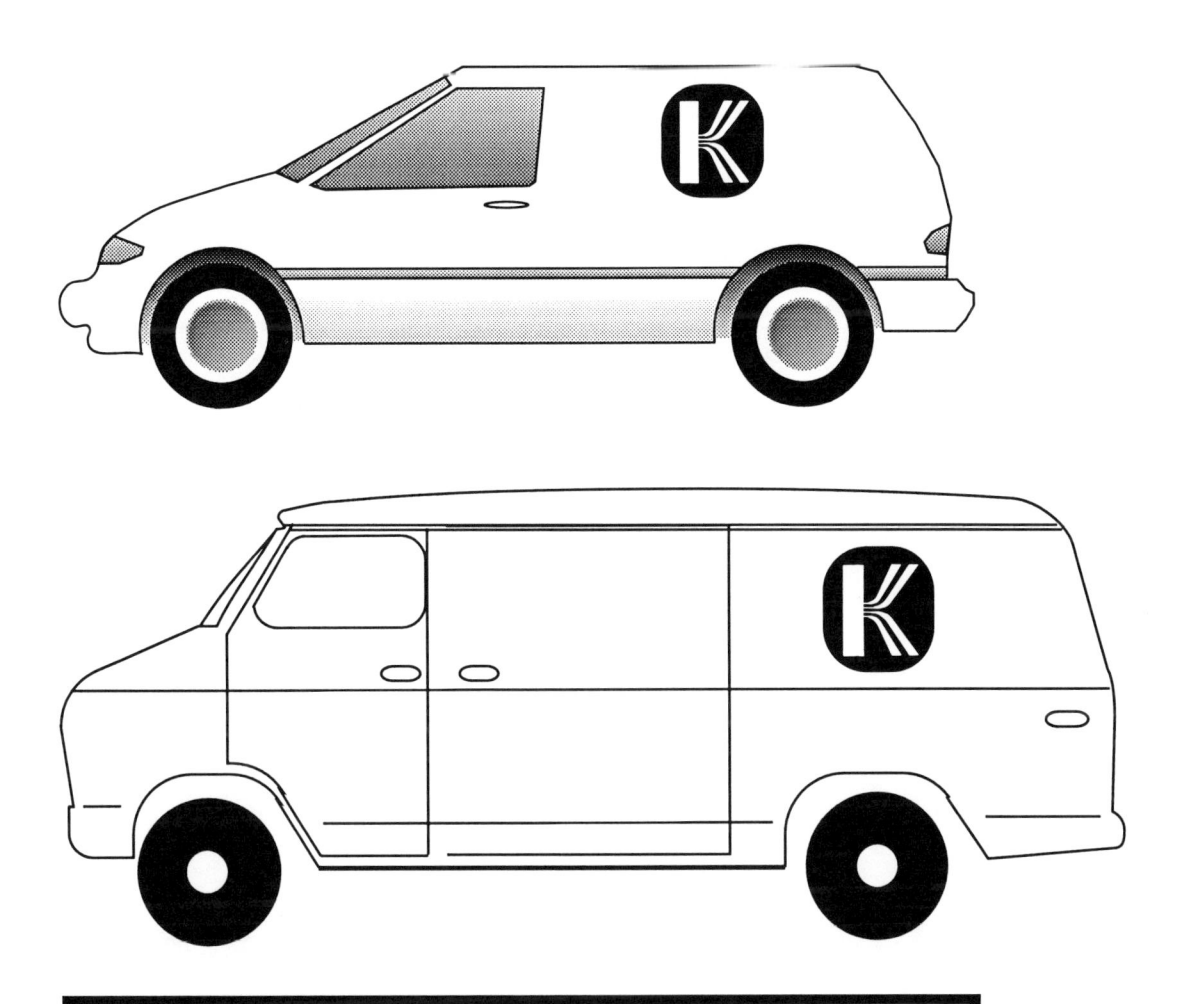

$50 off on Logo SuperPower

When you order the full Logo SuperPower package, you can get $50 discount just by saying "I bought Dave Carter's Book" over the phone when you place the order. Actually, there's just one more step in order to get the discount. We want to know that you *did* buy the book, so have this book handy when you place the order, so we can verify your purchase by a question we'll ask you. To order Logo SuperPower, call the number below.

Logo SuperPower is a product of Decathlon Corporation, 4100 Executive Park Drive, #16, Cincinnati, OH 45241 (800) 648-5646 or (513) 421-1938.

Part Four
Sample Logo Design Project

On the following pages is a step-by-step example of a mythical logo design project. The job begins with a description of the client, and also includes the design parameters. Then, each step of the design process is shown, concluding with the final logo and some of its applications.

    Although the project is not real, this is a very accurate representation of how a typical logo design project proceeds.

Chapter 15
The Pinnacle Corporation
Identity Program

Client information: The Pinnacle Corporation is the new name chosen for a bank holding company that intends to diversify into a variety of financial services, including real estate, insurance, brokerage, etc. The holding company is being formed by the merger of three existing banks. In addition, the company wants to keep itself open to other options for expansion in the future. Therefore, the logo should be applicable to any type business.

The design will have many possible uses: everything from business cards to signs to vehicles to packages. Since the logo will be reproduced in a large variety of sizes, it is imperative that the design reproduce well for all applications: from 1/4 inch up to several feet tall.

Since this is a new name created by a 3-way merger, with a totally new logo, there will be no need to retain any equity from any of the previous logos. Since each of the three merging partners had different corporate colors, there is no restriction on colors to be chosen.

The merger of the three banks was done from a position of strength, not one of weakness. Each of the banks brings some strong market positions to the newly formed holding company. The combined management is strong, and the merged entity should have a large share of market in its current locations.

The company has ambitions growth plans, both geographically as well as in number of services offered. The new identity should reflect that image. Management is very progressive, and the design should present a visual identity that is appropriate for a company that is a market leader.

Design parameters: The Pinnacle Corporation logo project presents a challenge to create a design that will reflect leadership, strength, growth and security. The word "pinnacle" means top, best, foremost, so a visual that reflects these traits should be considered.

The name "Pinnacle" will normally be displayed along with the logo, although there will be some cases in which the logo may stand alone. Due to the variety of uses (such as signage, checks, etc.) optional designs should be done so that the name can be used either at the side or bottom of the logo.

The initial nomenclature will be limited to "Pinnacle Bank." However, as the company grows, additional names such as Pinnacle Realty, Pinnacle Brokerage, etc. may be used. The design must allow for such future needs.

Since the design is to have a useful life of at least 20 years, it is important that the type be chosen carefully. Only "classic" fonts should be considered. Any "fad" type face will be quickly out of date.

For information purposes, the existing logos of the three merging partners are shown below. Since there is no "equity" requirement for this project, it is not necessary to use elements from any of these designs. However, in any project such as this, it is important to be aware of the past design history of the client.

FirstState Bank

Newport National

TSB&T
Trans-State
Bank & Trust

First round of proposed logos for The Pinnacle Corporation

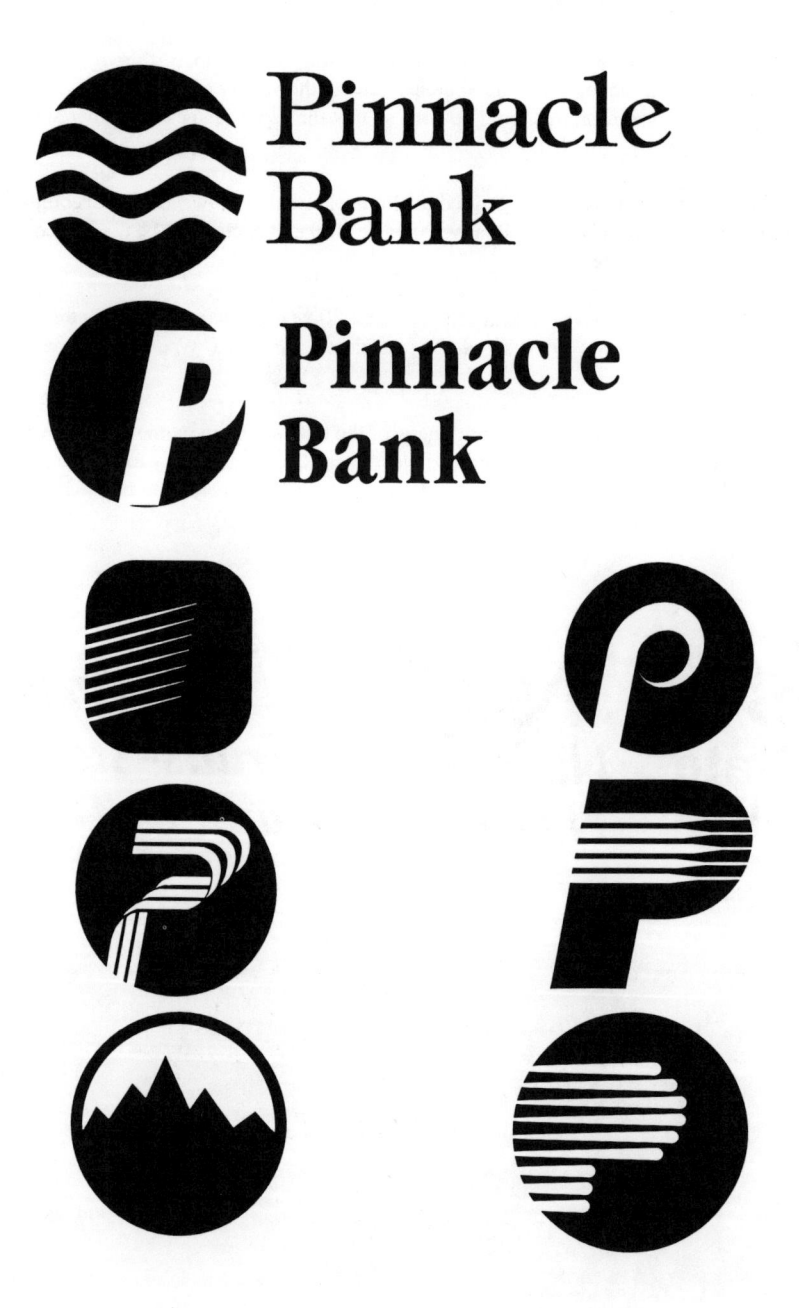

Pinnacle Bank

Pinnacle Bank

The designs on the left were shown to the client for our first presentation. We decided to show two of the designs with type, since the logo will normally be used with the name in place.

Our two favorite designs were those shown below, but after reviewing all the work shown on the opposite page, the client decided that he did not want to have a logo which featured the initial P.

We were directed to do new proposed designs which would all be somewhat abstract. So, we went back to the drawing board (or in this case, to the computer, since we don't have a drawing board any more).

Second round of proposed logos for The Pinnacle Corporation

We created a number of possible design to the client's specifications. At our next meeting, we presented the 17 designs shown below. For now, we decided to concentrate on getting a logo chosen. We'll work on the type aspect later. The client liked three of these, and asked to see them with the name in place in appropriate type faces.

Second client presentation made; Client's suggested revisions

These are the three logos which the client liked. We made presentations of each one with two different type faces. The client immediately chose the one he liked best, and gave us the final approval. our next step would be to show various applications for the design, which would include future divisions such as Pinnacle Realty, Pinnacle Brokerage, Pinnacle Properties, etc.

This was the client's choice for the final logo. His comment: "I like the look of the mountain effect. It visually expresses the name Pinnacle. I also like the strong bold type, and the italic look has a very progressive feel."

233

Final logo design
The Pinnacle Corporation

We presented the final logo in two forms: stacked (or vertical) on top, and the horizontal version, shown below.

Final letterhead set
The Pinnacle Corporation

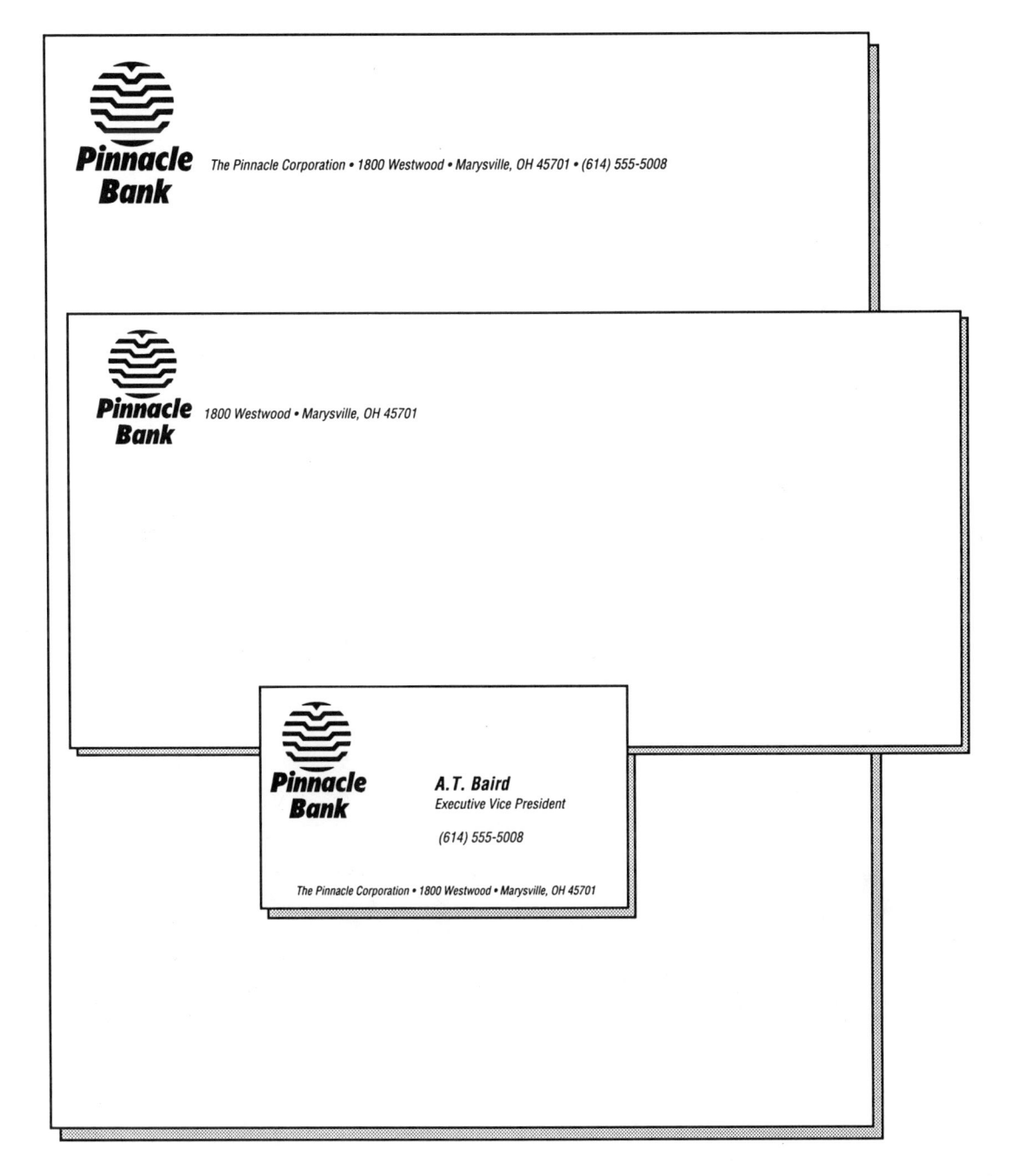

Pinnacle Bank — The Pinnacle Corporation • 1800 Westwood • Marysville, OH 45701 • (614) 555-5008

Pinnacle Bank — 1800 Westwood • Marysville, OH 45701

Pinnacle Bank

A.T. Baird
Executive Vice President

(614) 555-5008

The Pinnacle Corporation • 1800 Westwood • Marysville, OH 45701

Logo applications
The Pinnacle Corporation

We created examples of how the logo could be used for the bank's current needs, as well as for use in the future with divisions which are part of the firm's long-range plan.

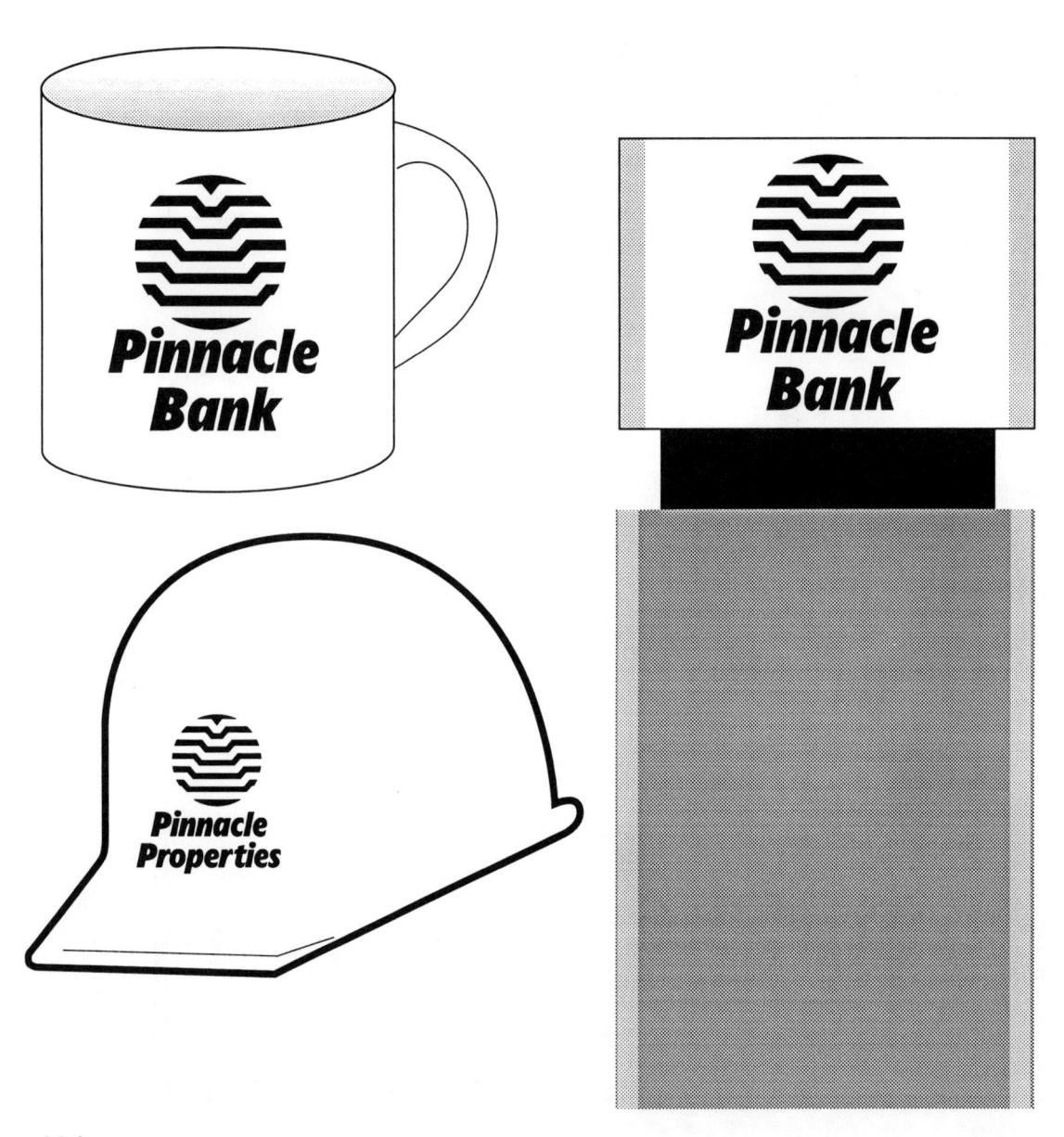

Pinnacle Properties

Pinnacle Realty

Pinnacle Brokerage

My Favorite Logos

Whenever I conduct a seminar on corporate logos, people invariably ask "will you show us some of the logos *you* designed?"

Even though nobody asked, I'm still going to show some of my best design work. The first two are from the B.C. era (before computers). All the rest were done on my Macintosh (using Logo SuperPower).

Kentucky Electric Steel Co.
designed 1968

Cardinal Federal Savings Bank
designed 1980

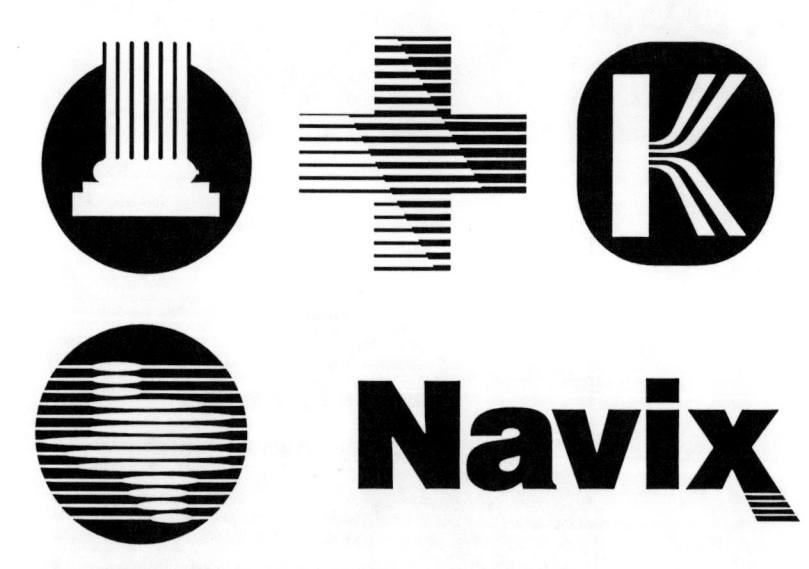

Logos shown above, top row from left: Kentucky Bank & Trust; Theparak Hospital (Bangkok, Thailand); Kodel (Jakarta, Indonesia). Bottom Row: Texas First; Navix Corporation. All were done using Aldus FreeHand and Logo SuperPower between 1990 and 1992.

David E. Carter

David E. Carter has produced more books on logo design and corporate identity than anyone else in the world. All of his 50+ books are in worldwide distribution and many are used in college classes in more than 20 countries.

He is president of David E. Carter, Inc., an identity consulting firm based in Ashland, Kentucky, with affiliate offices in Bangkok, Thailand and Jakarta, Indonesia.

Carter has created corporate logos and identity systems for more than 300 companies, and has presented corporate identity seminars on four continents.

Logo SuperPower™ and NameMax, his two software creations, are used by ad agencies, design studios and corporations around the globe.

Carter is also an accomplished writer for television. He produced more than a dozen comedy sketches for The Tonight Show Starring Johnny Carson, and he has won five Emmys for public TV programs he wrote and produced.

He is a graduate of the University of Kentucky School of Journalism and has a master's degree in advertising from Ohio University. He is currently enrolled in the MBA program at Syracuse University.

 David E. Carter is president of David E. Carter, Inc. P.O. Box 2500; 2155 Carter Avenue, Ashland, Kentucky 41105-2500. (606) 329-0077.

other books by David E. Carter

American Corporate Identity (8 volumes)
Corporate Identity Manuals
Designing Corporate Identity Programs for Small Corporations
Evolution of Design
Logos of America's Largest Corporations
Logos of Major World Corporations
Logos of America's Fastest-Growing Companies
World Corporate Identity (3 volumes)
Book of American Trade Marks (11 volumes)
How to Improve Your Corporate Identity
Designing Corporate Symbols
Logo International (4 volumes)
Letterheads (7 volumes)
International Corporate Design Systems

All these books are available from Art Direction Book Co. 10 E. 39th Street New York, NY 10016 (212) 889-6500.